THE SPIRITUALLY VIBRANT HOME

THE POWER OF MESSY PRAYERS, LOUD TABLES, AND OPEN DOORS

DON EVERTS

An imprint of InterVarsity Press
Downers Grove, Illinois

InterVarsity Press
P.O. Box 1400 | Downers Grove, IL 60515-1426
ivpress.com | email@ivpress.com

©2020 by Lutheran Hour Ministries

InterVarsity Press® is the publishing division of InterVarsity Christian Fellowship/USA®. For more information, visit intervarsity.org.

Scripture quotations, unless otherwise noted, are from The Holy Bible, English Standard Version, copyright © 2001 by Crossway Bibles, a division of Good News Publishers. Used by permission. All rights reserved.

All figures, unless otherwise noted, designed by Chaz Russo, data visualizations developed by Roxanne Stone and Alyce Youngblood, Barna Group; copyright Lutheran Hour Ministries.

While any stories in this book are true, some names and identifying information may have been changed to protect the privacy of individuals.

The publisher cannot verify the accuracy or functionality of website URLs used in this book beyond the date of publication.

Cover design: David Fassett
Interior design: Jeanna Wiggins
Images: house: © CSA Images / Getty Images
      another house: © CSA Images / Getty Images
      mid size home: © CSA Images / Getty Images

ISBN 978-1-5140-0790-7 (paperback) | ISBN 978-0-8308-4590-3 (casebound) |
ISBN 978-0-8308-3645-1 (digital)

Printed in the United States of America ♾

Library of Congress Cataloging-in-Publication Data
Names: Everts, Don, 1971- author.
Title: The spiritually vibrant home : the power of messy prayers, loud tables, and open doors / Don Everts.
Description: Downers Grove : IVP, an imprint of InterVarsity Press, 2020. | Includes bibliographical references.
Identifiers: LCCN 2019052308 (print) | LCCN 2019052309 (ebook) | ISBN 9780830845903 (print) | ISBN 9780830836451 (digital)
Subjects: LCSH: Families–Religious aspects–Christianity. | Families–Religious life. | Hospitality–Religious aspects–Christianity.
Classification: LCC BV4526.3 .E94 2020 (print) | LCC BV4526.3 (ebook) | DDC 248.4–dc23
LC record available at https://lccn.loc.gov/2019052308
LC ebook record available at https://lccn.loc.gov/2019052309

8 7 6 5 4 3 2 1 | 30 29 28 27 26 25 24 23

"In *The Spiritually Vibrant Home*, Don Everts provides an informative and empowering tool to maximize our relationships for gospel influence. He reminds us that spiritual vitality is shaped not primarily through institutional exertion but by our little personal orbits impacting people in meaningful ways. If you want to discover authentic pathways to get people connected to Jesus, let *The Spiritually Vibrant Home* inspire you and guide you."

Michael W. Newman, author of *Gospel DNA: Five Markers of a Flourishing Church*

"If you only have time to read one book this year on energizing your family's spiritual life, read this one. Since I finished *The Spiritually Vibrant Home*, I have found myself talking about the content and quoting it every day. I love the blend of quality research by the Barna Group and the excellent practical insight of Don Everts. You will find real hope and understanding to help your family thrive spiritually."

Jim Burns, president of HomeWord, author of *Understanding Your Teen* and *Doing Life with Your Adult Children*

"Everts has done it once again! He has woven together the great data-driven research of Barna with crisp biblical analysis and topped it off with illustrative material from his life that makes the possibility of passing on the faith within households come alive for the reader. Like all Everts's writing, I come away encouraged to live in ways that I can now see concretely."

Jim Singleton, Gordon-Conwell Theological Seminary

"Nothing drains the joy out of home quite like the stress of wanting to do it right. Don rescues his readers from duty and fear with low-barrier, accessible insights backed by solid research. Scripture and his own family story come together with a few simple practices to give us more hope for home, and for the spiritual vitality we find when our households welcome the messy, loud, and unpredictable adventure of friendship with Jesus."

Tim McConnell, pastor, author of *Happy Church: Pursuing Radical Joy as the People of God*

CONTENTS

FOREWORD

BROOKE HEMPELL

Senior VP, Research, Barna Group

The past few years my colleagues and I at Barna have been studying today's teens and youth: "Gen Z." I had become hyperaware that my kids were growing up in a very different world from my own childhood and that my husband and I would have to be highly intentional about shaping our kids' faith in order for them to thrive when they set out on their own. But neither of us had experienced a model of a healthy Christian home, so we worried that our default might not produce resilient faith in our children.

Our research team wondered about the dynamics of instilling and nurturing Christian faith in the home, so our partners at Lutheran Hour Ministries invited us to collaborate on an in-depth study of faith formation in Christian households. We wanted to understand the rhythms with which households of faith gathered: the *when*, *how*, and *why*. Who else was coming into the household on a regular basis, such as a grandparent or neighbor, and how they were participating in these regular rhythms? What spiritual practices were shared in the home, from praying and reading the Bible together to singing worship songs? What kinds of conversations were they having with each other, and how had these conversations shaped their faith?

Our hypothesis was that a vibrant faith is connected to being influenced by a variety of mentors. And, indeed, we found this to be true. Increasingly, household dynamics are not only defined by family members but also by the people we invite into our homes and routines. Throughout this study, we saw that *hospitable* households—those who regularly welcome nonfamily guests—fostered spiritual development through these interactions.

This study made it clear that Christians with the most vibrant, growing faith are emulating the New Testament church as described in Acts 2, whose deep faith valued fellowship and breaking bread, praying and reading God's Word together, and experiencing and demonstrating countercultural Christian love.

Hospitality, as well as faith formation, requires *intentionality*. The importance of fostering intimacy, sharing rituals, and having fun with household members—as well as friends and other nonfamily guests who become part of one's extended household—cannot be overstated. Yet these effects do not happen on their own; they happen through purpose and planning.

The Spiritually Vibrant Home unpacks the research and what it all means for our households. This book provides Christians with a roadmap to developing intentional rhythms that nurture their spirit, honor their heavenly Father, and pass on their faith to the next generation.

INTRODUCTION

WHY DO WE GET SO EMOTIONAL ABOUT HOME?

It was a warm Sunday morning last fall when Lilly started to cry. Everyone else in classroom 3205 grew silent as Lilly's voice cracked a bit, a few tears spilling down her cheeks as she shared the complex mingling of hope and disappointment she felt when reflecting honestly on the spiritual health of her family.

Eventually, she grew quiet and thoughtful, and the eyes of everyone in the classroom shifted back to me where I stood up front. At that moment a singular question floated through my mind: *Don, what have you gotten yourself into now?*

I've been leading classes on Sunday mornings for years. But I had never before led a class quite like this. Lilly's tears made me wonder for a moment if I had made a mistake.

Most classes I've taught start with clarity. Mark's Gospel gives us a clear picture of being a disciple of Jesus—let's study Mark together. There are some clear principles for how Christians can thrive in suburbia—let's consider those principles together. Proverbs gives us clear wisdom for how to navigate life—let's memorize some proverbs together.

I've been told the classes I teach tend to be a bit heady at times. I think the observation is meant as a gentle corrective (please remember we have hearts, too, Don), but I've mostly taken it as a compliment and continued to offer classes in which we start with clarity and I try to impart that clarity to everyone in the class in ways that are memorable and helpful. Suffice it to say, there have not been many tears.

Until last fall, that is.

WHAT DOES A SPIRITUALLY VIBRANT HOME LOOK LIKE?

Last fall I became involved in a research project that the Barna Group and Lutheran Hour Ministries (LHM) were embarking on together.[1] The goal of the project was to pull back the curtains on Christian households to find out what faith looks like in the everyday moments of life. The full findings would eventually be published in a monograph for leaders,[2] but last fall we just had the initial findings and a profound curiosity: What do spiritually vibrant households look like? And can households armed with that knowledge actually strive to become more spiritually vibrant?

This curiosity was so strong that I decided to start a year-long class starting not with clarity but with curiosity. I gave the class a vague title, "Households of Faith," and watched as forty people made their way into classroom 3205 on that first Sunday.

These forty people included physically tired parents of young kids, emotionally tired parents of teenagers, battle-tested grandparents, and a few single people who were wondering if the class would be relevant to them at all.

The first week of class I stood up front and confessed that I wasn't starting with much clarity but with strong curiosity. I told them not to think of it as a class but rather as a learning lab, and I invited everyone there to join me in holding the Bible in one hand and the Barna research in the other and exploring together what exactly a spiritually vibrant home looks like and how we could put that knowledge to use in our own homes.

That's exactly what we did. We met on twenty-one different Sundays over the next nine months. We studied eighty-three passages from the Bible and dozens of graphs and infographics from Barna. We asked lots of questions. Not just questions about the Bible and Barna but honest questions about our own households—those we grew up in and those we were now a part of shaping.

That's when the tears started to come. And it wasn't just Lilly. Lilly felt a mixture of hope and disappointment as she honestly assessed the spiritual health of her own young household: "I just don't feel like we're spiritually vibrant at all . . . more like spiritually dormant." But she wasn't alone. Martha, a mother of two and grandmother of three, felt a mixture of regret and empowerment as she honestly assessed her own parenting back in the day and the opportunities she has now as a grandparent. Mark felt a mixture of sadness and hope as he considered how dads in general are doing in Christian homes across the country (not that great) and how he could do more as a spiritual coach in his own home.

We all found there's something inherently emotional about considering the home. While the research findings were seemingly benign and the Scripture passages were somewhat familiar to us, there's something unavoidably nontheoretical about considering the home.

Here, I'll show you what I mean. Spend a few moments looking at some of the at-a-glance findings from the research that we looked at during our first month together (see fig. 0.1).

Perhaps, like some of the men in our learning lab, you are a father, and reading about the "small role" fathers tend to play in the home makes you angry. Or sad. Or disappointed. Whether or not you are a father, perhaps reading about fathers' small role stirs up regrets (or latent gratitude) about your own father's role in your household growing up. We felt those emotions too.

Or perhaps reading about "faith heritage" stirs up emotions about how the Christian faith was (or wasn't) handed on to you when you were growing up. We had lots of thoughts and feelings and reflections about our families of origin.

If you are a parent, reading about faith heritage might make you wonder how good a job you are doing at handing on the Christian faith to your own children. All of us parents in the room wondered those same things.

If you are single, reading a few findings about spouses and households may make you feel left out of the conversation once again, wondering why every Christian book or sermon or devotion seems to be centered on couples or families. The single folks in our learning lab wondered the same.

Or perhaps you are an empty nester and, like our faithful table of grandparents, you want to leave more of an imprint on your grandchildren but aren't sure if that is possible or how you would even begin to do that. Maybe reading about how isolated empty nesters can be makes you wonder if your chance at influence is over.

Perhaps these initial emotions make you wonder whether you should keep reading. That's basically what I was feeling after Lilly shared her heart with all of us and everyone turned back to look at me. *Is the home just too personal to assess? Is it too convicting to study the shape of spiritually vibrant homes? Is there any hope we can actually help our own imperfect households become more spiritually vibrant over time?*

Rather than shuttering the class that warm Sunday morning last fall and resigning ourselves to the status quo in our homes, we pressed on. We looked carefully at what the research reveals about the shape and habits of spiritually vibrant homes. We studied what the Bible reveals about God's design for our households and how helpful Jesus is in growing the spiritual vibrancy of households. And we held the Bible and Barna up like a mirror, getting honest about our own households.

AT A GLANCE

Generally, active households are spiritually active households and vice versa.

Shared meals, work, and play are common in households that also carve out time for faith interactions.

Faith formation is connected to and increases with hospitality.

Households that regularly host nonfamily guests are more likely to talk about faith, pray, or read the Bible together.

A majority of practicing Christians participate in spiritual conversations, prayer, and Bible-reading with their households.

Beyond the home, church attendance is also a common group activity, only behind eating out in frequency.

Practicing Christians occupy many kinds of households, primarily as nuclear families or in roommate contexts.

For the most part, Christians also live with people of the same ethnic background and religious identity.

Faith heritage impacts Christians' beliefs and practices for the long term.

Christians need influences outside their family of origin or household to grow in both theology and tradition.

Overall, spouses are the primary relationship that Christians interact with and confide in.

Unmarried adults have a more diverse mix of people on whom they depend, though mothers top their list.

Couple households, primarily made up of boomers and elders, are fairly isolated.

The routines of these older Christians tend to orbit their spouse, and half do not regularly welcome guests.

Kids become a catalyst for any interaction, including faith-related ones.

Homes with minors have broader communities, busier schedules, and more spiritual conversations.

Fathers play a smaller role than mothers in terms of both presence and influence in their households.

Teenagers' siblings are equally as involved as their fathers in meeting emotional and spiritual needs.

Spiritually vibrant households are characterized by fun and quality time.

Games, singing, reading, and sports are common group activities among households that Barna defines as *vibrant*.

FIGURE 0.1

Our consensus after nine months? Keep reading! There is real hope and healing power for all of us. We learned more about ourselves and our homelife than we thought we would. We were surprised and humbled and convicted and encouraged by what we saw in our homes and in God's Word. We created homework and tried new things in our homes. We shared the results with each other and laughed and cried. In the end, we saw God change our homes in ways small and big.

I'm glad we pressed on. And I encourage you to do the same. No matter what kind of home you grew up in, no matter what your home looks like right now, the truth is God made you to be a part of a spiritually vibrant household that grows more spiritually vibrant all the time.

ARE MESSY PRAYERS, LOUD TABLES, AND OPEN DOORS REALLY THAT POWERFUL?

One of the fruits of our messy learning lab is *The Spiritually Vibrant Home*. What you hold in your hands is not a memoir, a theological treatise, a recipe book, or a blog about life hacks. But it is reminiscent of each because the reality is our hearts and our faith and our houses are all thoroughly interconnected.

We'll begin our journey by exploring the spiritual significance of the mundane (chap. one, "Homelife") and reckoning with the somewhat surprising way the Bible talks about our homes (chap. two, "Households"). At that point (chap. three, "Vibrancy"), we'll pull back the curtains on spiritually vibrant homes and learn about the three everyday habits they have in common: messy prayers, loud tables, and open doors. In the last three chapters we will explore each of these household habits in greater detail, learning how we can nurture those habits in our very own homes.

Along the way we'll encounter a miraculously preserved ancient village, surprisingly large Israelite households, lots of insightful numbers from the research, and plenty of unremarkable but honest moments from my own journey. Some of these moments are a little embarrassing, but in the end this only increases my hope: it really is possible to have a spiritually vibrant home. Even for someone like me!

This whole process has given me hope for my own household and steps to take toward spiritual vibrancy. And that gives me the courage to invite you along for this journey to see what God's Word proclaims and the latest research confirms about we humans and our homes.

If you are still reeling from the less-than-perfect home you grew up in, keep reading. You may find that God has compassion and hope and healing for you.

If you are a frenzied parent who feels ill-equipped to pass on the faith, keep reading. You may find that God's recipe for spiritual vibrancy is much more attainable than you've guessed.

If you are single, keep reading. You may be surprised by how God defines a household, and you may feel empowered to take your important place in helping shape your own household and the households of others.

If you are an empty nester or grandparent wondering if your home is now resigned to quietness and boredom, keep reading. You may be thrilled by how hungry people are for your influence and discover practical ways to invest in your lasting legacy.

At the end of the day it doesn't matter what your age or stage of life is; there is great hope that comes from exploring how your heart, your faith, and your home are meant to work together. And that's exactly what *The Spiritually Vibrant Home* invites you to do.

In the end, I pray that just like me and Lilly and all of the imperfect learning-lab folks in room 3205, we will all know ourselves, our God, and our homes on a deeper level. May our own prayers become a little messier, our own tables a little louder, and our own doors a little more open. May we all experience the spiritual vibrancy God has for us and our homes.

HOMELIFE

RECOGNIZING THE SPIRITUAL SIGNIFICANCE OF THE MUNDANE

But as for me and my house,
we will serve the LORD.

JOSHUA 24:15

I was standing in my small, white kitchen staring down at a full trash can when I became a man. Often, it's only in retrospect that we recognize these significant threshold moments in life. That was definitely the case here. I'm sure I assumed, before walking into the narrow kitchen that morning, that I was already a man.

I was twenty-five, after all. And I had only two weeks before gotten married. My new wife, Wendy, and I had moved into this small mother-in-law house in Parkland, Washington, and we were both a few years into our professional lives working in campus ministry. But looking back, I don't think I really crossed that threshold into adulthood until I went to empty the trash one Saturday morning and saw something that stopped me in my tracks.

Unsuspecting, I had simply pulled out the trash to empty it. But looking down into the trash, I saw the unbelievable: yesterday's newspaper (this was back when we still had newspapers) and a few empty cans. My pulse increased. My brow furrowed. I called out, instinctually, "Wendy!" Wendy came around the corner to see what the cause of such urgency in my voice was. "What is it?" she asked.

"What is this?" I asked, with all the conviction and disappointment, I assume, of a strict school teacher. I was pointing down at the trash can.

Wendy looked confused. "What's what?" she asked, shrugging and trying to appear, I surmised at the time, as innocent as she could. I pulled out the newspaper and proclaimed (*declared*, might be a better term) the following:

"In. This. House. We. Recycle."

I know. Compassion for Wendy is very much in order here. You'll begin to notice this is a bit of a theme in our married life.

In my defense I was pretty passionate about doing what I could to tread lightly on the earth, and recycling (newspapers at the very least) was one way I had decided to do that. I really was shocked to see the newspaper and cans in the trash. And I really messed up in how I communicated that to Wendy. And she really was gracious to me. Today we laugh every time we retell this story from the early days of our married life.

My poor handling of the moment aside, this was a real moment. What kind of household were we going to be? Were we going to be a recycling household? It turns out this was the first of many questions we were going to ask about our common life together. A few months later we moved from Washington to Colorado, and this move brought with it a veritable storm of new domestic questions. Practical questions that got at real issues: Where will we live? How big of a table will we have? Will we have many guests? How do we arrange the living room? What will we do during the holidays? For entertainment? With our money? Will we have a television? What size screen? Where will our computer be? Pets? Roommates? Kids?

We were starting the adult work of creating and shaping our new household. Even though most of these questions had to do with our house (or apartment, to be more accurate during those early years), they were questions about much more than housing. These seemingly innocent domestic questions were ultimately connected to something much deeper: our values, our priorities, our hopes, our emotions, our relationships, our healing, and, in the end, our Christian faith.

People always make domestic decisions based on deeper values. It turns out this has always been the case. How we humans craft our domestic life is intricately connected to how we approach life itself.

DO WE PUT LOCKS ON OUR DOORS?

The word *house* may conjure obvious and familiar images in our minds (couches and tables, doors and windows, beds and chairs), but that doesn't mean there is something inevitable about the shape of our domestic life. Writer and historian Bill Bryson researched the entire human history of houses and homes and apartments and concluded that "nothing about this house, or any house, is inevitable. Everything had to be thought of—doors, windows, chimneys, stairs."[1]

Bryson spends 581 pages recounting the fascinating relationship between humans' values and priorities and how they shaped (and shape) their housing. Domesticity has always been an important part of our humanity. As Bryson reflects on millennia of humans and their households:

> Houses are really quite odd things. They have almost no universally defining qualities: they can be of practically any shape, incorporate virtually any material, be of almost any size. Yet wherever we go in the world we recognize domesticity the moment we see it. This aura of homeliness is, it turns out, extremely ancient.[2]

As Bryson recounts, a storm off the coast of Scotland in 1850 led to a striking reminder of exactly how ancient the questions of household really are. The storm raged for two days over the Orkney Islands. When it finally subsided, the locals realized that a large, grass-covered knoll they had always used as a landmark had been stripped of its grass coverings. Revealed underneath were "the remains of a compact, ancient stone village, roofless but otherwise marvelously intact."[3]

This ancient village, which came to be called Skara Brae, consisted of nine houses still holding many of their last occupants' household items. These contents, and the structure of the houses and village itself, tell us lots about the people who lived there. This is remarkable given the fact that the village was last lived in thousands of years ago. The shape of their houses (and their mundane contents) tell us much about these people.

In Skara Brae, for example, they found a drainage system in each home—with slots in the walls to wash away wastes. This small, mundane detail tells us something about what they valued—cleanliness perhaps? Every little domestic detail at Skara Brae was purposefully crafted by the original inhabitants and is worth noting:

- The walls were up to ten feet high—leaving plenty of headroom.
- Their floors were paved.
- Their doors had locks.
- They had built-in stone dressers and shelves and water tanks.
- They had covered passageways between the houses that led to a paved, open area where tasks could be done in a social setting.

Here's the thing: none of these details were inevitable. They were all purposeful and tell us something about the values and priorities and habits of the people who lived there. Consider, for example, the fact that all of the houses were the same size and built to the exact same plan. This mundane domestic detail tells us something about their values, perhaps "suggesting a kind of genial commune rather than a conventional tribal hierarchy."[4]

This remarkable find tells us that folks living thousands of years ago did the same thing I did while standing in my kitchen looking into my trash can: they made decisions about their homelife that were intricately connected to their values and hopes and fears and priorities. Even seemingly small housing decisions are important. Consider the fact that archaeologists found at Skara Brae one dwelling separated from the others. This dwelling was much like the others except for one tiny detail: the lock on the front door was on the *outside* of the door. Think about everything that implies. A small, domestic detail that tells us a lot. (I assume this was where they locked up people who refused to recycle their newspapers and cans.)

These days a trip to Home Depot may seem as far from your values and priorities and spirituality as possible, but the reality is how we set up and live in our housing matters desperately. It is central to the shape of our life. And for those of us who are Christians, seemingly mundane domestic matters turn out to be central to our discipleship as well.

DO HOUSEHOLDS MATTER TO JESUS?

As a disciple of Jesus, I take an interest in what interests Jesus. What matters to Jesus matters to me—or at least it should. And so it is noteworthy to me as a Christian that households seemed to matter to Jesus.

Consider the fact that Jesus used the household to describe his kingdom. Many of his teachings and parables about his kingdom drew strongly from domestic language and imagery, causing some scholars to conclude that the household is "the central image that informs Jesus's explication of the kingdom."[5] Jesus didn't talk about his kingdom with imperial or military pictures but with images from everyday households (fig. 1.1), with God as a father.[6] This has led some to conclude that Jesus' whole life and ministry "demonstrated a household concern."[7]

FIGURE 1.1

Jesus did not try to supplant the traditional household as we see in some other world religions and spiritual movements. Rather, Jesus embraced and valued the household, choosing individual homes as a central tool of his new kingdom. Much of the time Jesus spent in ministry was spent in the context of houses and families.[8] This domestic preference was purposeful and explicit.

It is significant that Jesus pursued his redemptive ministry in a household context. Mark's Gospel seems to emphasize this, showing us how Jesus was willing to speak to whole crowds but that his endgame was always to have people come closer to him, to sit down with him in homey proximity. This shows how reliable and effective the household context is as a sort of redemptive laboratory—a place where we can really be known and know others, a place of unhurried conversation.

This connection between discipleship and the household remained strong in the early church. As Michael F. Trainor points out in *The Quest for Home*, "The earliest Christians were members of households and gathered in houses to ponder the story of Jesus and its implications for their lives in the Greco-Roman culture in the late first century C.E."[9] The household became the "basic social unit of the church."[10]

So intertwined were the Christian life and the household that the earliest requirements for church leaders had to do with their domestic life. Do you want to know how to choose a good leader for your local church? The pastoral epistles are clear: look inside their home (see, for example, 1 Timothy 3:1-13). The mundane, domestic details of life (how someone handles finances, how they parent, how their household is doing) are signals to whether someone would make an apt spiritual leader of a church. They understood the everyday home is one of God's chosen contexts for working in his people's lives.

While God can (and does) interact with individuals in a vacuum, he often uses the household as a reliable laboratory for discipleship. Consider Paul's conversion. We tend to focus on the interaction Paul had with God on the road to Damascus—a bright light and a voice from heaven are pretty memorable. But remember it was actually in Judas's house on Straight Street that Paul's conversion really took seed. As Luke records the events, "Saul rose from the ground, and although his eyes were opened, he saw nothing. So they led him by the hand and brought him into Damascus. And for three days he was without sight, and neither ate nor drank" (Acts 9:8-9). God got his attention on the road, but it was three days in Judas's house on Straight Street where God's words began to work on Paul, where he clearly heard what he was supposed to do.

As I reflect back in life I can see that God has certainly worked in my own life outside of my home (through special times of prayer, lonely walks, retreats of silence, corporate worship services—plenty of Damascus Road moments), but it seems the most consistent place of life change in my past

FEELS LIKE HOME

The routines, activities, and relationships of a household all work together to create an atmosphere, a certain character or undercurrent that defines the home. When asked to describe their households, most Christians use positive—indeed, homey—language.

Comfortable: 69%
Loving: 67%
Safe: 65%
Peaceful: 55%
Casual: 54%
Joyful: 51%
Playful: 41%
Nurturing: 38%
Old-fashioned: 25%
Intellectual: 22%
Artistic: 14%
Messy: 14%
Tense: 9%
Crowded: 6%
Secretive: 6%
Sad: 4%
In crisis: 3%

n=2,347 US practicing Christian adult and teens, April 5–11, 2018.

CASUAL

INTELLECTUAL

ARTISTIC

IN CRISIS

LOVING

NURTURING

SAD

JOYFUL

COMFORTABLE

OLD-FASHIONED

SECRETIVE

PLAYFUL

SAFE

TENSE

MESSY

PEACEFUL

CROWDED

FIGURE 1.2

has been in that messy, humbling, in-your-face laboratory of the household—like when I was taking out the trash as a newlywed—more of a Straight Street moment.

This highlights the importance of the home and the overall atmosphere of the home. Do our homes have an overall atmosphere that is conducive to the discipleship work God wants to do inside us? The latest research underscores just how important the overall atmosphere of a home is. We'll get into the research in more detail in chapter three, but for now notice in figure 1.2 the words that are the most common descriptors of the atmospheres of Christian homes (with more common answers indicated with a larger font).

> **1.** Which words would you use to describe the atmosphere of your own household? Which two or three words would be the biggest?
>
> **2.** Which two or three words do you *wish* described the atmosphere of your home?
>
> **3.** In your experience, what changes the atmosphere in a home over time?

The atmosphere of our homes matters because this is where much of our discipleship growth occurs. Where has God most consistently formed my character, healed my heart, and taught me the values of his kingdom? In my home, through marriage, parenting, hospitality, close friendships, chores and routines and tragedies and parties and unhurried conversations and inviting people over for a meal.

It turns out the household is not only connected to our deeper values and priorities (as we see in Skara Brae), but it is also connected to God's real discipleship work inside of his followers (as we see in Jesus and the early church). As Tish Harrison Warren put it so memorably, "The crucible of our formation is in the anonymous monotony of our daily routines."[11] The household is the ideal place for us to work out our Christian discipleship.

WHAT ABOUT ME AND MY HOUSEHOLD?

This all means that we may need to reexamine the spiritual significance of our own mundane household moments. As Warren put it, "If I am to spend my whole life being transformed by the good news of Jesus, I must learn how grand, sweeping truths—doctrine, theology, ecclesiology, Christology—rub up against the texture of an average day. How I spend this ordinary day in Christ is how I will spend my Christian life."[12]

Just as in Skara Brae, our values and priorities will get worked out in these mundane domestic decisions and habits. With those we live everyday life with. Like Wendy and me working on our recycling (and communicating) habits on a slow Saturday morning. The latest research on spiritually vibrant homes shows this clearly. Notice in figure 1.3 the twenty-three separate activities that correspond with more spiritual vibrancy in a home.

WHAT MAKES FOR A VIBRANT HOUSEHOLD?

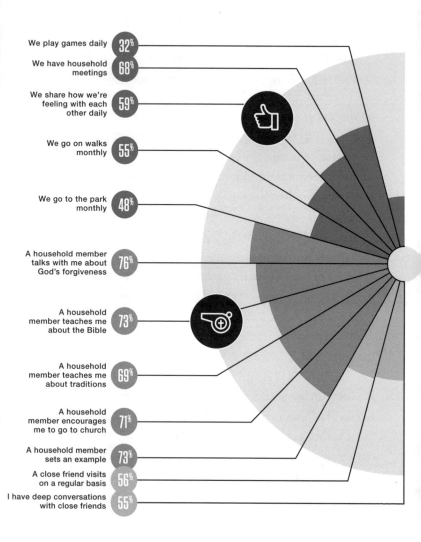

We play games daily **32%**

We have household meetings **68%**

We share how we're feeling with each other daily **59%**

We go on walks monthly **55%**

We go to the park monthly **48%**

A household member talks with me about God's forgiveness **76%**

A household member teaches me about the Bible **73%**

A household member teaches me about traditions **69%**

A household member encourages me to go to church **71%**

A household member sets an example **73%**

A close friend visits on a regular basis **56%**

I have deep conversations with close friends **55%**

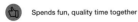 Spends fun, quality time together

 A spiritual coach is present

 Welcomes others

 Asks for help

 Members have a personal spirituality

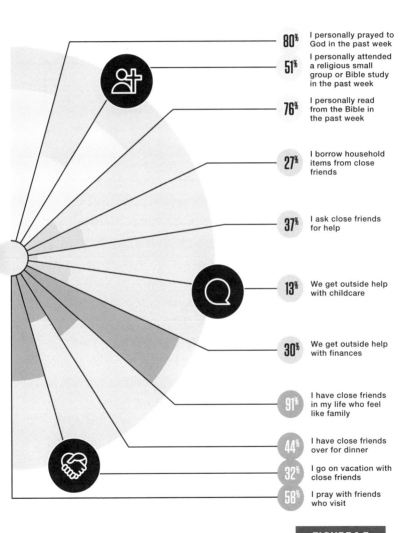

80% I personally prayed to God in the past week

51% I personally attended a religious small group or Bible study in the past week

76% I personally read from the Bible in the past week

27% I borrow household items from close friends

37% I ask close friends for help

13% We get outside help with childcare

30% We get outside help with finances

91% I have close friends in my life who feel like family

44% I have close friends over for dinner

32% I go on vacation with close friends

58% I pray with friends who visit

FIGURE 1.3

1. How many of the activities listed in figure 1.3 were present in your household growing up?

2. How many of the activities listed in figure 1.3 are present in your current household?

3. The research finds a correlation between these activities and spiritual vibrancy. What connections can you imagine exist between some of the more mundane activities and being more spiritually vibrant?

While there are a number of explicitly spiritual or religious activities that mark spiritually vibrant homes (like teaching about the Bible, praying with friends, or praying together), it is somewhat surprising how many of these twenty-three activities are mundane in nature (like going to the park monthly, going on walks, asking friends for help, playing games). Yet the research is clear: mundane household activities are spiritually significant.

We see the same dynamic play out in the Bible with Joshua and his household. We tend to think of Joshua's household proclamation in Joshua 24 as a leadership moment. After going in to possess the Promised Land, Joshua called all the leaders together for a covenant renewal ceremony to remind the tribes' leaders of the big picture: God gave them the land; when they crossed the Jordan River they were drawing a line. Joshua did have great leadership words that day:

> Now therefore fear the LORD and serve him in sincerity
> and in faithfulness. Put away the gods that your fathers
> served beyond the River and in Egypt, and serve the LORD.
> And if it is evil in your eyes to serve the LORD, choose this
> day whom you will serve, whether the gods your fathers
> served in the region beyond the River, or the gods of the
> Amorites in whose land you dwell. But as for me and my
> house, we will serve the LORD. (Joshua 24:14-15)

Sounds like a leadership moment, right? And it was. But consider
again how Joshua concluded this famous call to faithfulness:

> But as for me and my house, we will serve the LORD.
> (Joshua 24:15)

Joshua wasn't just a man of God. He was a man in a household.
And as such he needed to decide along with his household how
they together were going to live out their faith in the nitty-
gritty moments of life. It's worth noting that in the land they
were about to possess, homes were filled with small statues of
gods placed in niches in the walls. Joshua knew the everyday
domestic temptations they would face and so stood up with his
household to decide how they were going to live every day by
serving God.

A little bit like Wendy and me on that Saturday morning. I
wasn't just a disciple of Jesus as I looked down at my trash; I
was a part of a household. A household that needed to figure

out how it was going to recycle—and communicate. But is recycling too mundane to really have spiritual significance? Consider the questions Tish Warren poses for us:

> God made us to spend our days in rest, work, and play, taking care of our bodies, our families, our neighborhoods, our homes. What if all these boring parts matter to God? What if days passed in ways that feel small and insignificant to us are weighty with meaning and part of the abundant life that God has for us?[13]

What if all these boring parts matter to God? This question invites us all to examine the spiritual significance of our mundane domestic moments.

Just like the people who lived thousands of years ago in Skara Brae and the people who lived with Joshua in ancient Israel and the people who lived in the early church in Palestine during the Greco-Roman period, I, too, have a household. And how I create and shape my domestic habits matters immensely.

But how do we really know if all these boring household parts really matter to God? The Bible, it turns out, has a lot to say about households.

HOUSEHOLDS

UNPACKING HOW THE BIBLE SEES OUR HOMES

These are the names of the sons of Israel
who came to Egypt with Jacob,
each with his household: Reuben,
Simeon, Levi, and Judah, Issachar,
Zebulun, and Benjamin, Dan and
Naphtali, Gad and Asher.

EXODUS 1:1-4

I was nervous the first time Wendy took me to meet her family. We had only been dating for a few months, and although I had already met her mother and stepfather (briefly while they were visiting our college campus), it's something else entirely to be brought home to "meet the family."

And that's exactly what we were doing. On the drive north from Tacoma, Washington (where our college was), to

Mt. Vernon, Washington (where Wendy had grown up), Wendy made sure I really appreciated that we were heading to a *family party*. She uttered these two words as if they were special. So special that I needed to be sure to appreciate where exactly we were going.

I was nervous enough already, but as Wendy told me again what to expect, my nerves began to grow. I think I had only been half listening when she first invited me—something about a family party, meeting her relatives—I may have tuned out the rest.

But now, as we were driving north, Wendy had my full attention. And the questions were starting to flow. "So, Wendy, exactly how many people are going to be at this family party?"

"Close to fifty," Wendy replied calmly as if that were the most obvious size for a family party.

I was shocked. "Wait. Exactly how big is your family?!"

"Really big. I told you this, Don. This is a *family party*, remember?"

I sort of remembered. As we drove north, my mind was trying to stretch around these new expectations. "Yeah, I remember, but . . . they are *all* going to be at this party?"

"Right. Remember, I told you my entire extended family gets together once a month?"

"Every month? All of them?" The introvert in me was starting to twitch a bit.

"Yes. Don, I told you this, right?"

She had told me that. But I was only half listening. Also, I don't think my own family experiences really prepared me to understand what she was saying. My family, just the five of us, moved a lot growing up, so I didn't really know my extended family. I had vague memories of a trip to a family reunion in Minnesota when I was in elementary school—we met lots of people and ate lots of Swedish rosettes and gaped at all the snow. But mostly it was just my immediate family that I knew: just the five of us. Nothing in my experience prepared me for Wendy's *family party*.

And what a party it was. There were lots of people: young, old, and in-between. There was lots of food (this was my first, but not last, time having the famous dish known as "Grandma's rice"). And there was lots of conversation—everyone lived nearby, so there was no I-rarely-see-you-so-I-don't-really-know-what-to-talk-about awkwardness. Everyone was at home.

I met lots of people, shook lots of hands, ate lots of food, and endured the kindhearted teasing that comes with being the boyfriend who's been brought home to meet the family. And I saw Wendy moving among them like a fish in water, loving it all.

Halfway through the party I sat down on a couch just to take it all in and realized I was sitting next to Wendy's stepfather, Bob. "Quite a thing, isn't it?" he asked me, motioning with his hand toward all the people and conversation and food. I agreed. Then Bob went on to tell me that he had grown up an only child.

"I wasn't really prepared for all this the first time I came to one of these parties." I agreed again.

As we sat watching the festivities a realization began to dawn on me: being in a relationship with Wendy meant being in a relationship with all these people. It was a package deal. Wendy wasn't just Wendy. She was also a part of this extended family. Which meant . . . what? What is it like to relate to an entire extended household like this?

As I sat pondering these questions one of the aunts started playing the piano, a gaggle of people formed around her, and they all began singing familiar songs together, no sheet music necessary. It was a joy to watch them singing, Wendy right in there with them. When Uncle Eddie got out a saw and bow (yes, a hand saw that he played with a violin bow, bending the saw to get different notes, and no, I am not making this up), I had to smile and shake my head. I liked dating Wendy. And I thought, *I'm really going to like dating Wendy and her extended household.*

In this way, dating (and eventually marrying) someone in a large, extended family prepared me to understand an important biblical truth: God relates to us not just as individuals but as households.

God cares quite a bit about our households. This is something we see throughout the Bible. Whether God was relating to a nation (in the Old Testament) or a church (in the New Testament), households mattered to God. While it is true, of course, that God sees each human as an individual with an identity and dignity unto themselves (think of the sublime reference we have in Psalm 139 about the careful individual attention each human receives from God), it is equally true from the biblical evidence that God sees and pays attention to our households.

The Bible explicitly mentions "households" over two thousand times in the Old Testament and over one hundred times in the New Testament, to say nothing of the many implicit references to households. The Bible has quite a lot to say about God and his relationship to our households (fig. 2.1).

But before we explore what the Bible has to say about our households it's important that we clarify what exactly the Bible is referring to those twenty-one hundred times when it brings up a household. Is it referring to a small, nuclear family, like the one I grew up in? Is it referring to a large, extended family

FIGURE 2.1

like Wendy grew up in? Or is it referring to something else entirely? What exactly are the biblical writers referring to when they bring up the household?

WHAT EXACTLY IS A HOUSEHOLD?

The two words the Bible uses to talk about households are the Hebrew word *bayit* (used in the Old Testament) and the Greek word *oikos* (used in the New Testament). These are the same words used when referring to the structure and also to the people within that structure. While there are other words to explicitly specify the people within the structure (words for "family," for example), it is interesting that the primary words used for the structure and the people within the structure are the same. As the ruins of Skara Brae illustrate, there is a real, inextricable connection between the people and where and how they live together.

So in the Bible, a "household" is a group of people living their life together.

But don't let that simple description cause a modern picture of a small, nuclear family in a detached home to pop up in your mind—like the family I grew up in. That is a foreign concept to the Bible and would be anachronistic for us to read back into the texts. Rather, when the Bible talks about households, it is referring to large, extended households. This extended household would include family members as well as others connected to the family. This is something closer to what I saw at that first *family party* with Wendy.

Consider households in the Old Testament, for example. While the average American family today consists of 2.58 people, the average Israelite household would have consisted of fifty to one hundred people.[1] Consider the roll call of Jacob's household that appears in Genesis 46—his household consisted of seventy people. This is something like the extended household I met when Wendy brought me to meet her family and is similar to the extended families we see as the norm in many other countries in the world even today.

Who are all these people in these large households? Brenda Colijn writes this in her brief summary of family in the Bible:

> The ancient Hebrew family included husband and wife, their children (and if their sons were married, their wives and children), the husband's parents, the husband's brothers and their families, the husband's unmarried sisters, and other relatives. It might also include multiple wives and concubines, with their children and their children's families.
>
> Besides those related by blood or marriage, the household would include servants and slaves, guests (who were bound to the family by the obligations of hospitality), and sojourners (aliens resident in the household and its ongoing protection, often employees of the household).[2]

In ancient Israel all of the people of a household would generally reside in a cluster of housing units forming a residential compound of sorts.[3] So when you read about a household in the Old Testament, you are reading about an extended family, plus others that are connected in an intimate way to their family, all living life together. An extended family *plus*. Something very different from our notion of a nuclear family. As Colijn puts it, "The modern American notion of family is more narrow, individualistic, privatistic, and exclusive than the biblical one."[4]

The same is true of the many households referenced in the New Testament. By the time of the New Testament, Greco-Roman culture had produced significant changes in how society was structured, but one thing had not changed: households were still as large and extended as they had been throughout Israel's history. A regular household in the time of the New Testament would have included "the extended family, servants or slaves, clients, and guests."[5]

Such was the norm in ancient Greece that on some occasions writings refer to a "whole household" or "complete household," which included nonrelated people beyond just the extended family, to distinguish it from households that, oddly, only contained relatives.[6] The fact is the household was the basic unifying structure in Greco-Roman culture during the time of the New Testament. As Wayne Meeks observed in his book *The First Urban Christians*, "The household was, of course, much larger than the modern family and would have included relatives, slaves, freedmen, hired workers, and sometimes tenants, as well as colleagues in trade and crafts."[7]

In Jesus' day did these large extended households live under one single roof? It is likely that the Israelite practice of households living in clusters of close homes continued (with some architectural and cultural adaptations) into Greco-Roman times. The large, organized Roman city did bring new architectural and domestic norms into play during the time the New Testament was being written, but extended households *living together* were still the norm throughout most of the time the Bible was being written.[8]

All this tells us that whenever the Bible refers to a household (something it does *a lot*), it's most likely a reference to an extended family plus others who are attached in some meaningful way to that family. And these folks were living life together.

WHO IS IN MY HOUSEHOLD?

But what exactly is a household today? With such a significant biblical category (twenty-one hundred references) we want to be thoughtful about how all those texts apply to our current lives. Obviously, there are not always going to be contemporary equivalents to practices we read about in the Bible. (When was the last time you washed your guests' feet before a dinner?) But in order to understand and apply the Bible in our own day, we need to be thoughtful about how to apply what we read there to our lives today. (Washing feet was an act of humble, kind service. How can we engage in acts of humble, kind service today?)

Therefore, before delving into what the Bible says about households, let's ask, Do we have a contemporary equivalent of the Bible's household in our day? As we've seen, a household in the Bible is an extended family—plus others who are attached in some meaningful way to that family—living life together. Do we have something like that today?

Family is close. But what we mean by *family* is generally too narrow and limited and insular. My own family growing up would not be an apt equivalent to the Bible's household.

Roommates definitely captures some of the elected nature of biblical households (travelers, colleagues, guests), but roommate situations these days tend to be more short-term and sometimes transactional in nature.

Some people's experience of *church* may get close. But what we refer to as church today is usually something too large and geographically spread out to match up with households in the Bible.

A *small group* can get close, especially if whole families are involved in it—not just a member of the family who goes off to their own small group. But small groups tend to be too ancillary to the actual family or not regular enough to allow folks to be living life together.

We Christians talk a lot about *community* and perhaps even mean by that term something akin to the biblical household, but it's hard to tell since community is such a vague, amorphous category much of the time. Lots of us

Christians use that word, but we mean all sorts of different things when we use the word.

I have had experiences with *teams* that overlapped quite a bit with what the Bible refers to as a household. But most teams don't actively involve the family, multiple generations, or living life together.

The fact is we don't have any single English word today that gets at exactly what the Bible is referring to as a household. So, what if we do this the other way around?

What if we take the Bible's word (*household*) and the Bible's understanding (a household is an extended family—plus others who are attached in some meaningful way to that family—living life together) and ask, *Who is in my household?*

If I were to reflect on my own life through the biblical category of household, I would have to say my whole household is made up of my core household plus members of my extended household (fig. 2.2).

My *core* household would include

- my nuclear family (my wife, Wendy, and our three kids: Simon, Teya, and Victor)

- my mom (Nancy lives with us)

My *extended* household would include

- a few of the wonderful, local friends who "feel like family" because of how often they are at our house and the

number of holidays and life events we share (Cypress is
one example; Bosede would be another)

- the Mackys (close friends, Chris and Sarah and their two
kids, Anna and Peter, who moved into our neighborhood
so that we could live life together on a pretty regular basis)

- a significant, and at times evolving, group of my children's friends. The more significant a friendship becomes,
the more it feels appropriate to say they are actually functioning as part of our extended household.

So, using the Bible's understanding of households, a map of my
whole household today would look something like figure 2.3.

FIGURE 2.2

It is new for me to think in this biblical category. This question, *Who is in my whole household?* is a new question to ask. While there is no strict definition to go by, I would say I can loosely define my own household as I have in these two sets of bullet points. How about you? What would your whole household map look like?[9]

Obviously, households will look different for different people. And one person's household will undoubtedly change

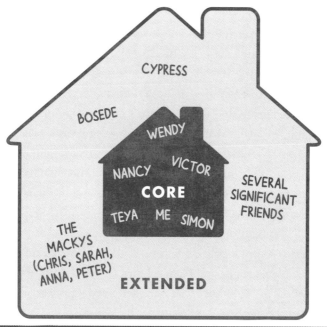

CYPRESS

BOSEDE

WENDY

VICTOR

NANCY

CORE

SEVERAL
SIGNIFICANT
FRIENDS

TEYA   ME   SIMON

THE
MACKYS
(CHRIS, SARAH,
ANNA, PETER)

EXTENDED

FIGURE 2.3

over time. But if you were to list who is a part of your household right now, who would you list in the core? Who is part of your extended household? Perhaps like our friend Cypress, you are an active part of *a couple* of households: Cypress currently lives alone and is not only an active part of our lives but is also active in the household of another family, the McDonalds. This is not uncommon. I know several empty nesters and retirees and grandparents who are active members in a few different households and who take their role in those different households quite seriously.

Now, is everyone, in some way or another, in a household, as the Bible thinks of households? Not necessarily. There are people in our culture who are not meaningfully connected or living life with anyone else. More than a quarter of adults in the United States live alone, and it is not uncommon, as we'll see later, for people to live where no one regularly comes into their home.[10] What psychiatrists call "chronic loneliness" is very common in modern American life, and although most patients suffering from it prefer the diagnosis of depression to that of chronic loneliness, the phenomenon is significant and dangerous.[11]

So it is definitely possible for people to be so cut off from family, from neighbors, from friends that they are not in a household as the Bible understands it. Even if they go weekly to a church service (participating in the household of God), it's possible to be so insulated that they are not functionally in a household. After all, social scientists have found we're not just "bowling alone"; we're also going to church alone.[12] So, no, not everyone is functioning in a household as the Bible understands households.

But *can* anyone be in a household? As the Bible understands households, yes!

This is one of the refreshing qualities of households in the Bible: there is a meaningful place for everyone who wants one. There is a place for you.

If the model for a household is the modern-day nuclear family, many of us are left out (roommates, people living alone, empty nesters). But with the Bible's model of an extended household, there is a place for everyone. Part of the beauty of a biblical household is that, by definition, it provides a place of belonging to people who would otherwise be living life alone, like widows and travelers for example.

I recognize it might be imprecise to try to import an ancient biblical structure (the household) into our contemporary context. Societal norms and ways of approaching family and housing obviously change from culture to culture and from age to age. But it is instructive to try to picture exactly what the Bible is referring to when it speaks of households. It is important to contemplate our own lives and relationships through the biblical household lens and contemplate who exactly is in our household. And here's why that's so important: the Bible speaks of households *a lot*.

WHAT DOES THE BIBLE SAY
ABOUT HOUSEHOLDS?

We can't unpack every single one of the twenty-one hundred biblical uses of *household* here, but when we do a survey of all these occurrences there are actually three major themes in the Bible related to households that stand out.

Theme 1: God sees households. I have to admit I'm so used to reading everything through an individualistic lens that I often miss this recognition of households. For example, Jacob brings his eleven brothers to Egypt to help them survive during the famine, right? Well, no. As we read in the verse at the beginning of this chapter, "These are the names of the sons of Israel who came to Egypt with Jacob, *each with his household*: Reuben, Simeon, Levi, and Judah, Issachar, Zebulun, and Benjamin, Dan and Naphtali, Gad and Asher" (Exodus 1:1-4, emphasis added).

I read that verse in the Bible and see twelve men walking into Egypt. But I'm wrong. This is not uncommon for those who grow up in individualistic rather than collectivistic cultures. As E. Randolph Richards and Brandon J. O'Brien describe this phenomenon in *Misreading Scripture with Western Eyes*, "Our individualistic assumptions affect our reading of Scripture in many ways, some of them more serious than others. Because individualism goes without being said in the West, we can often get the wrong idea of what an event described in the

Bible might have looked like. This can lead to the more serious problem of misunderstanding what it meant."[13]

I have to admit this happens to me. For example, I read in the Bible that when someone is faithful, God is careful to bless them. Well, not exactly. We have numerous examples where the story plays out as it did for Obed-edom, who was willing to store the ark of the Lord. As the Bible tells it, "The ark of the LORD remained in the house of Obed-edom the Gittite three months, and the LORD blessed Obed-edom *and all his household*" (2 Samuel 6:11, emphasis added).

I read in the Bible that God called a unique group of people, the Levites, to a special priestly service. And he blessed these individuals because of their service. Well, not exactly. As the Bible tells it God gave the Levites special food and said, "You may eat it in any place, *you and your households*, for it is your reward in return for your service in the tent of meeting" (Numbers 18:31, emphasis added).

While our own more individualistic lens may cause us to miss this emphasis in the Bible, it's always been there. God does see us as individuals. But he also sees us as households (fig. 2.4). What exactly does this mean? This means that God not only sees me and cares about me, but he also sees and cares about my household: my marriage with Wendy, our relationships and life with our kids. Perhaps it even means that God sees and pays attention to the way we widened our tent to bring my mom, Nancy (and her husband, Buzz, before he passed away), to live with us. Does God also see and pay attention to both Cypress's and Bosede's influence in our household and our influence in their lives? Does God care that the Mackys decided to move a couple of blocks away so that we could live our lives together? Does he pay attention to how our kids (who are a little older) bless the Macky kids (who are a little younger) and vice versa? Perhaps God even sees and notices that the Mackys' new dog, Dream, gets along with our beloved Chihuahua, ChiChi?

THEME 1
God sees
households.

FIGURE 2.4

Perhaps it seems I'm overstating the matter. Some of these domestic details seem too pedestrian to really matter, but the Bible's record is unambiguous: God sees and cares about households. Why? Consider the second biblical theme related to households.

Theme 2: Households often rise and fall together. While it is not a hard-and-fast rule that the behavior of one member of a household will affect everyone within that household, *often* this is the case. Sometimes this is wonderful. Think of the description of a godly woman that appears at the end of Proverbs. There is a glad recognition that her behavior affects her whole household:

> She rises while it is yet night
>   and provides food *for her household*. . . .
> She is not afraid of snow *for her household*,
>   *for all her household* are clothed in scarlet.
>   (Proverbs 31:15, 21, emphasis added)

But households don't just tend to rise together, they also tend to fall together. Consider Korah, who rebelled against Moses and Aaron. Korah's attempt at rebellion wasn't just a bad move for him but for his whole household, "As soon as he had finished speaking all these words, the ground under them split apart. And the earth opened its mouth and swallowed them up, *with their households and all the people who belonged to Korah and all their goods*" (Numbers 16:31-32, emphasis added).

The actions of one person can affect their entire household—often dozens of people. This household reality informs much of the wisdom literature in the Bible. For example, we're not only told that greed does harm to the heart of the greedy—"Such are the ways of everyone who is greedy for unjust gain; it takes away the life of its possessors" (Proverbs 1:19)—we're also told that it does harm to the greedy person's household—"Whoever is greedy for unjust gain troubles *his own household*" (Proverbs 15:27, emphasis added).

THEME 1
God sees households.

THEME 2
Households often rise
and fall together.

FIGURE 2.5

We see this same dynamic in the New Testament. Paul is grateful for the hospitality and generosity of Onesiphorus, so he prays that "the Lord grant mercy *to the household of Onesiphorus*, for he often refreshed me and was not ashamed of my chains" (2 Timothy 1:16, emphasis added). Paul prays over Onesiphorus's *whole household* because of Onesiphorus's actions.

While telling his disciples that they would be treated the same as he was, Jesus appealed to this household truism, "If they have called the master of the house Beelzebul, how much more will they malign *those of his household*" (Matthew 10:25, emphasis added).

Throughout redemptive history we see this same theme: households tend to rise and fall together (fig. 2.5). This is an important reality to reckon with. My faith (and faithfulness) is not just my own; it affects everyone in my household. In a similar way, Bosede's unique gifts don't just bless the people in her family; they are also a blessing to those in my own household. And Wendy's grace and ability to help people process their life is a game changer for all of us.

The latest research gives us a modern-day illustration of this dynamic. As you can see in figure 2.6, most households have a shared faith. Notice that while moms tend to have the greatest impact on the faith of those in a household, many others (including grandparents, friends, and other relatives) also have an impact on the faith of those in the household.

THE FAITH FAMILY TREE

Most households have a shared faith

The majority of practicing Christians inherited their faith from someone in their household of origin

However, a significant minority admits they are still Christians despite the faith they grew up with.

59%

Yes, someone passed their faith down to me

23%

I'm a Christian despite the sort of Christianity I saw in my household growing up

15%

No, my Christianity as an adult is not because of a person in my childhood household

11%

Yes, someone explored faith at the same time I did

2%

Other

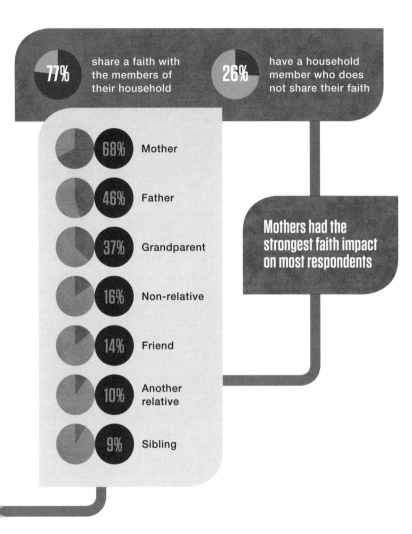

77% share a faith with the members of their household

26% have a household member who does not share their faith

68% Mother

46% Father

37% Grandparent

16% Non-relative

14% Friend

10% Another relative

9% Sibling

Mothers had the strongest faith impact on most respondents

n=1,116 US practicing Christian adults who say they became a Christian after birth, April 5–11, 2018.

FIGURE 2.6

1. Which of the five given answers in figure 2.6 best describes how you "inherited your faith"? Describe your own faith heritage in greater detail.

2. Describe the person who had the strongest faith impact on you when you were growing up.

3. Whose faith are you impacting in this season of your life?

It is both sobering and exhilarating to recognize and reckon with this biblical theme that households tend to rise and fall together. But as significant and noteworthy as this theme is, it might not even be the most important theme about households in the Bible. Consider the third theme.

Theme 3: God works through households. Again, I tend to notice when God chooses an individual and works through that individual for his grand redemptive purposes. These names easily come to mind: Noah, Abraham, Ruth, David—all individual people that God worked through to change the world. But the reality is God also often chooses to work through the household. Again, this theme runs throughout the Bible; we just haven't always had the eyes to see it.

For example, through Noah God kept humanity from being totally wiped out in the flood, right? Well, he actually did that grand work through a household: "Go into the ark, you and your whole household, for I have seen that you are righteous before me in this generation" (Genesis 7:1). As theologian

Simon K. Varghese reflected on this moment in redemptive history, "The family/household was the center of God's act to save humanity and the earth from total destruction by the flood. The growing web of corruption and violence led all the families on the earth, except Noah's family, to judgment by the flood."[14]

Or take another example: God began to form a people in this fallen world through one man, right? Well, yes and no. God called Abraham, to be sure. But God's redemptive work of creating a people was ultimately to be accomplished through a household: "I have chosen him that he may command his children and his household after him to keep the way of the LORD" (Genesis 18:19).

We see this same theme in the New Testament. God not only saves and redeems individuals for his kingdom purposes, but it seems that he also saves and redeems whole households for his kingdom purposes.

We have multiple accounts of whole households being saved: the Philippian jailer's household (Acts 16:31-32), the Capernaum official's household (John 4:53), Lydia's household (Acts 16:15), Crispus's household (Acts 18:8). Whether these whole household conversions are incidental (one individual's experience of faith *happened* to spread to the rest of the people in their household) or purposeful (God sovereignly *called* an entire household to faith), the theme is noteworthy. God calls and works through whole households (fig. 2.7).

No wonder then that from very early on the word people used to refer to God's redeemed people, this new church of Jesus, was *household*. It seemed natural enough for them to refer to this new structure as "the household of faith" (Galatians 6:10) or "the household of God" (Ephesians 2:19). This use of the term underscores how significant households were in the minds and hearts of the New Testament community.

This also causes me to reflect differently on my own household. When I lived in a roommate household, I mostly

THEME 1
God sees households.

THEME 2
Households often rise
and fall together.

THEME 3
God works through
households.

FIGURE 2.7

thought about recreation: What are we doing on Friday night? As a parent I'm tempted to think about protection: How do I keep my children from the fallen world around them while nurturing them as faithfully as I can? But as a member of a household I'm invited to think about purpose: How does God want to use my household for his purposes in the world?

The answers to this question could be pedestrian (in this family, we recycle) or exotic (for spring break we're going as a family to work in an orphanage) or relational (when we have people over, we put down our screens and welcome and engage with them). What a refreshing question to ponder: How does God want to work through my household?

It's one thing to ponder how God wants to work through *me*. Paul's words in Ephesians seem to invite me to consider that question, "We are his workmanship, created in Christ Jesus for good works, which God prepared beforehand, that we should walk in them" (Ephesians 2:10). I read that and wonder, what works has God prepared for me? But in light of the biblical theme of God using whole households, the pronoun Paul used (*we*) really jumps out. This verse causes me to ponder how God wants to work through my whole household. What collective impact does God want to create through *us*?

If God really wants to just relate to me as an individual, that's one thing. But if God really wants to relate to me and my whole household (a little like dating Wendy and her extended family), then that's something entirely different. What exactly does it look like to relate to God as a household? And, more to the point, what does it look like to do that well?

It turns out this is a powerful question that we can actually answer.

3

VIBRANCY

PULLING BACK THE CURTAIN ON SPIRITUALLY VIBRANT HOMES

By wisdom a house is built,
and by understanding it is established;
by knowledge the rooms are filled
with all precious and pleasant riches.

PROVERBS 24:3-4

I first heard about Gene Thomas when I was a college student. Various speakers and Bible study leaders in the campus ministry I was a part of would tell stories about Gene with an unmistakable sense of reverence in their voices. The stories were impressive and instilled in me a sense of respect and almost awe toward this Christian hero from the past.

Some of these stories brought Gene to life in my imagination and began to shape a picture of what a faithful campus minister could be like:

- Back in the day, Gene had started local chapters of our campus ministry on dozens of college campuses across several Rocky Mountain states—all while working a full-time job for a real estate company!

- Gene would walk the streets of Boulder, Colorado, during the Jesus Movement in the 1960s and 1970s and get into the most amazing spiritual conversations with people—so many people were coming to faith in Jesus that they held regular baptisms at a nearby reservoir!

- Gene could unpack Jesus' parables in a way that drew in hundreds of people who were hearing about Jesus for the first time! (I eventually located several old cassette tapes with recordings of some of his teaching—even through the scratchy, old tapes his simple, profound, engaging teaching style came right through.)

- Gene raised the money to buy a remote retreat center in the Rockies—college students came from all over to hear more about Jesus!

Other stories brought Gene and Gerri's (his wife) household to life in my imagination and began to shape for me a picture of what a faithful Christian home could be like:

- Gene and Gerri had a huge house next to the campus and constantly welcomed college students into their home to experience warm hospitality and learn about Jesus. They had even taken the lock off their door so that the college students knew they could come over whenever they needed something!

■ Gene and Gerri regularly hosted huge dinner parties for dozens of college students, the kids' friends, and neighbors. Often people would wind up sitting all over the floor because the many chairs and couches were full!

■ Gene and Gerri regularly employed homeless people to work around their house so that they could develop some work experience, healthy habits, and a résumé. The way I heard it, one month they were hiring people to build a rock wall in their backyard, the next month they were hiring a different group of people to take it down!

By the time I graduated and was working for this same campus ministry, I had heard so many of these stories that I was repeating them myself to inspire college students and shape their own picture of what Christian faithfulness could look like and what a faithful Christian home could look like.

In short, Gene and Gerri became spiritual heroes of mine.

And then something extraordinary happened: our campus ministry asked Wendy and me to move to Boulder, Colorado—the same city Gene and Gerri had done much of their ministry in. It was something to be walking the same streets Gene had, to be doing kingdom ministry on the same campus Gene had, to bring students up to the retreat center Gene had established all those years ago.

And then a wonderful day came: Gene and Gerri invited me over to their house. Gene was well into his eighties, and our campus ministry had asked me to do a series of interviews with Gene and capture, in book form, some of the stories of his and Gerri's ministry.[1] I had contacted Gene about the project and he heartily agreed, inviting me to come over to their house— the house of Gene and Gerri Thomas!

As I pulled up to the huge home hidden away in an old neighborhood right next to campus, I couldn't help but think, *I can't believe I get to go in the house where it all happened!* I knocked and a student let me in, led me to a den, and then went to get Gene. To be honest, as I sat waiting, my eyes taking in the bookshelves that lined every wall, I was mostly excited to *hear stories* about Gene and Gerri's hospitality and radical generosity and teaching exploits from back in the day. And I did. But what surprised and delighted me was that I also got to see it all still happening that day.

You see, as Gene and I sat in two comfy, high-back chairs talking about their ministry that had happened over fifty years ago, there was a constant flow of people through the house. Students still came and went, Gene greeting each of them by name. Gerri came in and joined us for a while, she and Gene enjoying telling the stories together.

At one point a man shyly stood in the entryway to the den. When Gene noticed him, he exclaimed happily and called him over, asking him about his trip to the hardware store. The man reached in his pocket and produced the change from his purchases and Gene waved it away: "Keep it for now; I'm sure we'll be needing you to head back for more supplies on the project." I looked at the man's general appearance and realized that Gene and Gerri were *still* employing people down on their luck to help them get back on their feet.

What a privilege it was to get to hang out inside the house of Gene and Gerri. To see firsthand how they lived their life. At the end of that first conversation, Gene offered to pray. He began to pray in that deep, calm voice of his, "Oh Father, you are so good to us . . ." Gene's nearness to and affection for God was unmistakable. That one moment of shared prayer in the den altered my own prayer life.

I walked back to the car that first day feeling as if I had been given a precious gift. To get to see inside the household of spiritual heroes is indeed a rare gift. And the more I understand households from a biblical perspective, the more grateful I am for those unhurried afternoons inside Gene and Gerri's house. As we've seen, the household is important in the life of a Christian, so getting to see inside their house to see how their strong faith affected their everyday domestic habits and decisions was truly inspiring and instructive.

This is why I am so grateful that through careful research it has actually become possible to pull back the curtain on strong households of faith across our country, just like Gene and Gerri's. And what we learn while sitting inside those homes is both inspiring and instructive. A precious, rare gift indeed.

HOW DO YOU LOOK INSIDE SOMEONE'S HOME?

In 2018 Lutheran Hour Ministries and the Barna Group undertook a three-year, collaborative research project.[2] The first area of research was "spiritual conversations in the digital age," which paved the way for everyday Christians to rethink how they engage in spiritual conversations.[3]

The second area of research has to do with "households of faith"—specifically turning the lens of research toward how the Christian faith "is being nurtured and lived out in private—with the people who come and go from under Christians' roofs."[4]

FIGURE 3.1

The goal of the new research project was to get a view inside the Christian household, and that was accomplished through a series of qualitative in-person interviews followed by quantitative surveys of 2,347 practicing Christians (fig. 3.1). The resulting data and research findings can be found in *Households of Faith: The Rituals and Relationships That Turn a Home into a Sacred Space.*[5]

Both the interviews and the surveys were guided by simple curiosity: "What does faith look like on a day-to-day basis, in practicing Christians' most familiar relationships, personal environments or unobserved hours?"[6] In other words, how does this redemptive laboratory of the household actually work?

In order to study whole households and not just families (getting as close as possible to what the Bible refers to as a household), questions weren't merely focused on someone's family but rather the people who are a regular part of someone's life—including those who "feel like family." As you can see in figure 3.2, questions were asked to get at people's "extended household members." As the researchers put it,

A cornerstone of the concept for this study is that household dynamics are not only defined by occupants and family members, but by the people we invite (or don't invite) into our homes and routines. This study refers to these familiar faces as extended household members. Many practicing Christian respondents regularly host visitors at least several times a month. These guests—

HOUSEHOLDS AND THEIR CLOSEST FRIENDS

DO YOU HAVE ANY PEOPLE IN YOUR LIFE WHO ARE SO CLOSE THAT
THEY FEEL LIKE FAMILY?

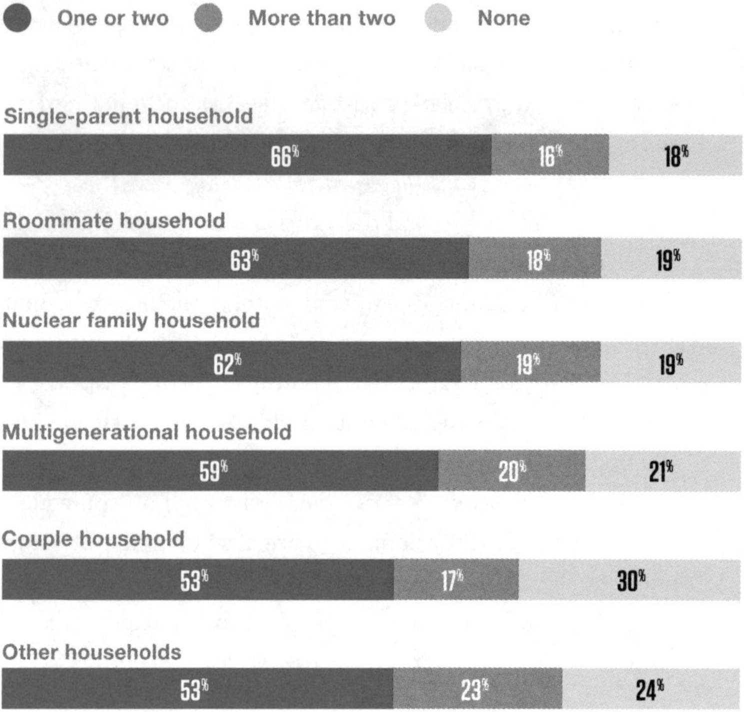

● One or two ● More than two ● None

Single-parent household

| 66% | 16% | 18% |

Roommate household

| 63% | 18% | 19% |

Nuclear family household

| 62% | 19% | 19% |

Multigenerational household

| 59% | 20% | 21% |

Couple household

| 53% | 17% | 30% |

Other households

| 53% | 23% | 24% |

n=2,347 US practicing Christian adults and teens, April 5–11, 2018.

FIGURE 3.2

usually relatives (69%), but also close friends, neighbors, significant others, exes, caregivers and more—have a degree of influence on residents.[7]

While all research has limitations, getting to observe statistically significant patterns and differences leads to significant insights about the group being surveyed. In this case, the surveyed group wasn't just the general population. It wasn't even a group of self-identified Christians. The group surveyed was a group of *exemplars*—practicing Christians whose faith is very important to them (fig. 3.3). In fact, in order to be included in

Practicing Christian Households

FIGURE 3.3

the survey, respondents had to "strongly agree" that their faith was very important to them.

So this research isn't just pulling back the curtain on a random group of households, rather we are given the gift of being able to peer into the habits and practices and feelings of strong, practicing Christians. In other words, we are getting to spend unhurried time in the households of hundreds of people like Gene and Gerri.

DO THESE HOUSEHOLDS ALL LOOK THE SAME?

There was a great deal of diversity in the households surveyed. As you can see in figure 3.4, there were several different household types among those surveyed. (You can find definitions of each type in appendix 3, "Definitions.")

This is noteworthy. While the Cleavers of *Leave It to Beaver* may have been seen as a prototypical family at one point in our history, they are certainly not anymore. Today there is a great diversity of household types. The nuclear family may be a staple on television or in the movies, but it is wrong to assume that most people live in such a household. Reality is much more varied and diverse.

Today's households are quite diverse, and the reality is "the average person will progress through various types of households during their lifetime."[8]

So, the research pulled back the curtain on a wide variety of household types. And those households were found in a

DISTRIBUTION OF HOUSEHOLD TYPES IN THIS STUDY

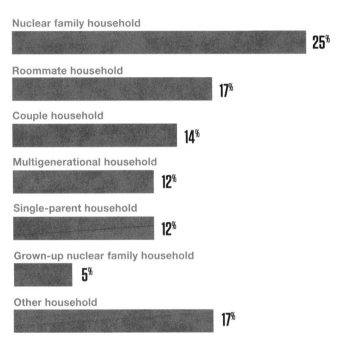

Nuclear family household
25%

Roommate household
17%

Couple household
14%

Multigenerational household
12%

Single-parent household
12%

Grown-up nuclear family household
5%

Other household
17%

USING VARIOUS APPROACHES TO POPULATION ESTIMATES, BARNA PROJECTS
THAT BETWEEN ONE IN TEN AND ONE IN FIVE PRACTICING CHRISTIANS
LIVE ALONE WITHOUT ANYONE ELSE IN THEIR HOME. PLEASE SEE THE
METHODOLOGY IN THE APPENDIX FOR A DETAILED DESCRIPTION OF HOW
AND WHY THE STUDY FOCUSED ON MULTIPERSON HOUSEHOLDS, AS WELL AS
PROFILES OF THE HOUSEHOLD TYPES.

n=2,347 US practicing Christian adults and teens, April 5–11, 2018. Total does not add up to
100 percent due to small overlap in single-parent and multi-generational groups.

FIGURE 3.4

TYPES OF NEIGHBORHOODS HOUSEHOLDS OCCUPY

Urban   Suburban   Rural   Small town

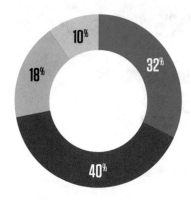

n=2,347 US practicing Christian adults and teens, April 5–11, 2018.

FIGURE 3.5

HOUSEHOLD TYPE, BY GENERATION

Teens • Millennials • Gen X • Boomers • Elders

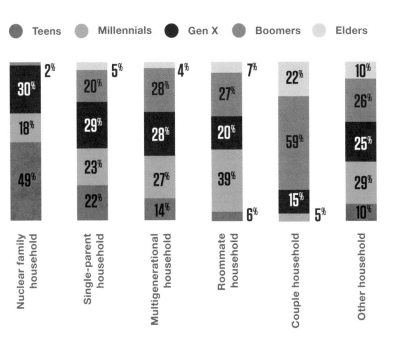

Nuclear family household
2%
30%
18%
49%

Single-parent household
5%
20%
29%
23%
22%

Multigenerational household
4%
28%
28%
27%
14%

Roommate household
7%
27%
20%
39%
6%

Couple household
22%
59%
15%
5%

Other household
10%
26%
25%
29%
10%

n=2,347 US practicing Christian adults and teens, April 5–11, 2018.

FIGURE 3.6

wide variety of neighborhoods. As you can see in figure 3.5, these households were in urban, suburban, rural, and small-town settings.

Those who participated in the surveys also represent a wide variety of ages—from teens up to elders (those born in 1945 or earlier), as you can see in figure 3.6 (see also 3.7).[9]

It is important to note that researchers set specific quotas for a variety of these demographic factors so that their statistical analysis could give us a statistically representative look at what is happening inside the households

Practicing Christian Households

Diverse Households

FIGURE 3.7

of *all* active Christians *across the United States* whose faith is very important to them (fig. 3.8).

WHAT DO WE SEE INSIDE SPIRITUALLY VIBRANT HOMES?

When I was in Gene's house, I learned all sorts of things about him and his household. I saw him interact with his wife, learning something about their marriage and household routines. I was given a tour of Gene's extensive library, which lined all the walls, learning quite a bit about their value of reading

Practicing Christian Households

Diverse Households

Statistically Representative

FIGURE 3.8

and education—especially when it came to the Christian faith, the topic of most of the books.

I also got to see Gene and Gerri interact with a few of the university students who were boarding at their home as well as the man who was working for Gene. I even had the privilege of seeing Gene at prayer in his den and got to hear him talk about the Bible quite a bit. It was one thing to hear about Gene and Gerri as distant heroes, but it was quite another to get a glimpse into their household to see how their faith affected their mundane domestic habits.

The same is true in the research. It's one thing to know that there are Christian households out there that have a strong and active faith, but it's quite another to have extensive interviews and surveys that allow us to spend time looking inside their homes.

The research findings teach us quite a bit about people's marriages, life habits, faith practices, conversations, parenting, hospitality, and more. Through the findings we get to see people at play, at work, at meals, and just hanging out.

And while there were a variety of fascinating and useful lessons learned while spending time in these strong Christian homes, one large finding rises above all the others in significance. In short, these exemplar Christian households *regularly participate in applying spiritual disciplines, engaging in spiritual conversations, and extending hospitality.*

The presence of these three distinct, observable household habits corresponds to what the researchers call greater "spiritual vibrancy." The absence of any or all of these three habits is a risk factor and corresponds to less robust Christian discipleship. In practical terms, if you spend time in a spiritually vibrant Christian household, you will see people applying spiritual disciplines, engaging in spiritual conversations, and extending hospitality.

Or, put more memorably, you will see messy prayers, loud tables, and open doors (see fig. 3.9).

The Spiritually Vibrant Home

| MESSY PRAYERS | LOUD TABLES | OPEN DOORS |

FIGURE 3.9

What, exactly, are messy prayers? In the findings, "applying spiritual disciplines" refers specifically to the household habits of praying together daily and reading the Bible together weekly. And what are loud tables? "Engaging in spiritual conversations" refers specifically to the household habit of talking with each other about God and faith weekly. "Extending hospitality" is the habit of regularly welcoming nonfamily guests into the home. That's what open doors refers to.

While each of these three "vibrant variables" was found to be fruitful and helpful within a Christian household, where *all three* were present the researchers saw something special. As the researchers observed, good things happen because of each of these household habits individually, but when all three are present, all of those good things are multiplied. Where you have messy prayer, a loud table, and an open door, you have a spiritually vibrant home.

IS THERE HOPE FOR MY HOUSEHOLD?

As those in my learning lab found out over the last year, there is something simultaneously exciting and frustrating about pulling back the curtain on spiritually vibrant homes. Hearing that there are three simple household habits that help produce spiritual vibrancy is inspiring and exciting. But contemplating your own household and its current habits related to spiritual disciplines, spiritual conversations, and hospitality can be humbling, embarrassing, and even frustrating.

I must admit that when I drove away from Gene and Gerri's house that first time, I was conflicted: I loved what I had seen, but I wondered whether I could ever have such a household myself. The feeling in that household was undeniably attractive. It felt like a warm, beautiful outpost for the kingdom of God. But how could I ever have such a household?

I lived in a small condo, after all. Gene and Gerri's huge, multistory house was just out of my reach. And I was an introvert who came from a somewhat isolated family of origin. Was there any hope I could someday shape and grow a household to be something like what I had experienced at Gene and Gerri's place?

The research suggests the answer is yes. As Rosaria Butterfield put it so memorably, "God can make magic in all kinds of faithful households."[10]

This is what's so encouraging and hopeful about these research findings: anyone can choose to pursue spiritual vibrancy. It doesn't matter if you have a large home or a small apartment. It doesn't matter if you live in the city or the country. It doesn't matter if you are in a nuclear household, roommate household, a single-parent household, or a multi-generational household. It doesn't matter if you are single or married. It doesn't matter if you live alone or with others. It doesn't matter if you grew up in a strong Christian home or not. The research suggests that any of us can pursue the habits that actually lead to spiritual vibrancy.

This isn't me trying to be inspirational, this is what the data suggests. In the technical language of the researchers, "Rituals and relationships have a meaningful impact on faith formation and can be replicated regardless of a household's category or context." Or, as they put it another way, "For the most part, spiritual vibrancy is not determined by unchangeable characteristics, but by things any Christian can improve."[11]

Pretty fancy, technical language for what we read in the wisdom literature of the Bible. As the proverb at the beginning of this chapter encourages us,

> By wisdom a house is built,
>   and by understanding it is established;
> by knowledge the rooms are filled
>   with all precious and pleasant riches.
>   (Proverbs 24:3-4)

What does it take to build a vibrant house (a house filled with all precious and pleasant riches)? It takes wisdom and understanding. And it turns out pulling back the curtains on spiritually vibrant homes has gifted us with some very specific wisdom and understanding that any of us can use to help build and establish our own homes.

MESSY PRAYERS

HELPING OUR HOUSEHOLDS RELATE TO GOD

These words that I command you today
shall be on your heart. You shall teach
them diligently to your children....
You shall write them on the doorposts
of your house and on your gates.

DEUTERONOMY 6:6-7, 9

All three of my kids liked being tucked in at night when they were children. This is a pretty normal gig: make sure teeth are brushed, talk a little about the day, pray for them, and give them hugs and kisses. This simple routine was going along just fine until my youngest, Victor, started making requests. Specifically, about the prayer part of being tucked in.

The first request had to do with volume. You see, I never really developed a habit of praying a memorized prayer with my children (Now I lay me down to sleep . . .) but rather just prayed impromptu prayers for them. As it turned out, by the time Victor came around, a fair amount of the time I was praying these prayers silently. I would place my hand on their head or hand, close my eyes, and pray silently for them.

The day eventually came when Victor was not okay with this. He interrupted my silent praying, "Daddy, you have to pray out loud."

I smiled and assured Victor that there are all sorts of different ways to pray, including praying silently. God hears us no matter what language we speak or whether we are speaking the words out loud or not. It was a pretty compelling bit of practical theology if you ask me. Victor didn't buy it.

"But I can't hear you if you pray silently."

He did have a point. So I started praying for him out loud on the nights I was tucking him in. The only problem was that this new habit made me realize that my silent prayers had been sort of a mix of praying, thinking, and trying not to fall asleep. Having to vocalize the prayers shined a light on how imprecise and vague and incomplete some of my nighttime prayers had been.

This problem came to a head when Victor (who, it turns out, has no problem asking for exactly what he wants) exclaimed one night after my simple prayer, "That's it?" His disappointment was clear.

I asked him if he wanted me to pray more. He sure did. "Mom prays way more than you."

Ah, there it was. My wife, Wendy, who has a much more mature prayer life than I, tucked in Victor as well, and he had grown accustomed to *her* prayers.

I couldn't believe I was having my prayer life challenged by my youngest son. I immediately grew defensive. But eventually I grew curious. *My prayers are okay, aren't they? What more would I pray for than what I was? How could I join with my son in talking to God at night in a more robust way? What would we talk to God about? What should we talk to God about? What do I ask God for? What do we tell God?* I was surprised by my struggles in this area.

After all, I had been a college minister for fourteen years and was a pastor in a local church. I knew how to pray with college students. I knew how to pray with struggling parishioners at my church. I knew how to gather a staff team together in meaningful prayer. I related to God personally and gathered together with lots of different people to relate to God together.

But for some reason I struggled to relate to God together with my son. Household prayer was tougher for me. As I leaned on Victor's bed, struggling for words at night, plenty of justifications came to mind: *I've been praying with people all day. Wendy just sets the prayer bar too high. I'm kind of tired at night. I don't have distinct memories of my dad praying with me.* But all along I couldn't deny that I was pretty sure relating to God as a family was a normal thing. In fact, I had a sense that the Bible paints a pretty clear picture that we are supposed to relate to God as households. My sense was right.

ARE WE MEANT TO RELATE TO GOD AS A HOUSEHOLD?

At times there is such an emphasis (rightly) placed on the local church as an important place of Christian growth, prayer, and worship that we can (wrongly) begin to assume a sort of sacred-secular split in life. Church is where sacred and spiritual things like prayer and worship and Bible study happen; home is where normal, domestic things like meals and chores and bedtime happen.

If those within a household are a little uncomfortable or shy or new at relating to God, it can be tempting to simply relegate all spiritual practices to church and feel you don't have to attend to them within your household. This can be lived out in different ways.

- Three young professionals become roommates, but even though they are all Christians, they never pray together or look at the Bible together unless they are in their small group at church—which they all go to. They relate to God together at small group but never at home.

- A young father who did not grow up in a Christian home has no muscle memory for how to pray together with his own children and so relegates that activity to church. *As long as I make my kids go to church*, he figures, *I am doing my duty as a Christian parent*.

- A Christian couple goes to church together, but other than mealtime prayers, they never pray together or open the Bible together. They know plenty of couples who don't even go to church together, so they feel that they are actually going above and beyond as a Christian couple.

It turns out this is a very different picture of a household of faith than the Bible paints. Throughout the Bible, God makes it clear that his people are intended to relate to him *as* households *in* their household.

Consider Moses' words on the Plains of Moab. Right before crossing the Jordan into the Promised Land the Israelites gathered around Moses to receive, anew, God's words of instruction on how he wanted them to relate to him and be his people. Right there at this threshold moment, God gave them foundational words that invited them into a living relationship with him: "Hear, O Israel: The LORD our God, the LORD is one. You shall love the LORD your God with all your heart and with all your soul and with all your might" (Deuteronomy 6:4-5).

This is a beautiful call to have a living relationship with their God. But what were the very next words God delivered through Moses? "And these words that I command you today shall be on your heart. You shall teach them diligently to your children.

. . . You shall write them on the doorposts of your house and on your gates" (Deuteronomy 6:6-7, 9).

This living relationship with God was to have a household shape to it. From the very beginning God invited households to relate to him as households in their households. Prayer and contemplating God's words were meant to be domestic activities. This had implications for all in the households but especially for the leaders of a household. As Colijn points out, "Religious commitments made by the head of the household involved the whole family. For example, Joshua spoke for his whole family when he said that he and his house would serve the Lord (Josh. 24:15). In early Old Testament times, the family was the center of worship."[1]

For the ancient Israelites this meant that parents were "responsible for conveying the family's faith in God to sons and daughters, through words and actions."[2] In essence the ancient Israelite household served as a religious community, passing spiritual traditions on through instruction and worship.[3]

When the tabernacle came into use and eventually the temple was built, there was a (right) emphasis on the role of the temple in relating to God, but the Israelites (rightly) never allowed the temple to replace their call to relate to God as a household in their household. As Colijn points out, "Even after the temple was built, however, families continued to observe Passover; perform circumcisions, marriages, and funerals; observe the dietary laws; and engage in religious instruction. Teaching the law to one's children was one of the obligations of the covenant."[4]

This basic understanding of the household as a place to relate to God together with one's relatives and extended household continued into the time of the New Testament church. In fact, the structure of the early church (house churches) was based on the household, and much of the life of the church took place in households, including evangelism, baptism, teaching, the Lord's Supper, and Christian education.[5] It is meaningful that during the Reformation catechisms were written to be used for faith formation within the household.

WHICH IS BETTER: A NEAT FURNACE OR A MESSY FIREPLACE?

There is something simultaneously exciting and scary about this. The sacred-secular split that is present at times in our Christian culture may not be too biblical, but it is quite neat. As a parent, all I have to do is make sure my kids go to church. Check. My role as a Christian parent is done. The church will take care of the rest. As a roommate, all I have to do is try to get my other roommates to go to small group with me. Check. My role in the household is done. The small group will take care of the rest. As a Christian spouse, all I have to do is go to church with my spouse. Check. As a Christian grandparent, all I have to do is get my kids and grandkids to come to church on Easter and Christmas Eve and Mother's Day. Check. Check. Check.

You can see the appeal, I'm sure. The sacred-secular split is neat and clear, and it relieves us of the inherent messiness that comes with relating to God together with others. The difference between this neat model and the biblical model seems to me to be similar to the difference between a furnace and a fireplace.

If you want to heat your home, there's nothing as convenient and easy as having a furnace. All you have to do is set the little dial on the thermostat to your minimum heat, and the machinery takes care of the rest. If it gets too cold, the furnace kicks on and the heat rises. Once you've set the temperature on that dial, you don't have to give the heating of your house any more thought. You can see the appeal.

Relegating our relationship with God to the church works in much the same way. All I have to do is set the minimum temperature (I just need to get my kids or my housemate to church), and I don't have to do anything else. The church takes care of the rest.

The biblical model is much messier and more time-consuming. Kind of like heating your home with a fireplace. Fireplaces are beautiful and captivating and almost magical. But boy, do they take time and energy. Not only is it tricky to start a fire, but once it's going your job isn't done. You have to constantly tend to a fire: adding more wood, stirring the coals, making sure there's enough air getting to the wood. You can never leave a fire for too long. And, let's be honest, fireplaces really can be messy: ashes floating, smoke rising, sparks flying.

Owning the household as a central place for relating to God is messy and time-consuming in much the same way. It takes constant tending, produces some messes, and can never be left unattended for long.

But even though I hate messes, I have to admit there's something so captivating and *alive* about a fireplace. By contrast, have you ever heard anyone say, "Remember that time we turned the thermostat to 70 degrees?" Fireplaces are magical and have a way of drawing everyone together in memorable ways. And such is the case with households that relate to God together.

While the ease of the sacred-secular split has its appeal, the Bible is clear that we are meant to relate to God as households. It's to be the fireplace, not the furnace. And the research supports this.

WHAT CAN WE LEARN ABOUT RELATING TO GOD FROM SPIRITUALLY VIBRANT HOMES?

The first of three household habits that corresponds with greater spiritual vibrancy within the household is "applying spiritual disciplines"—what we're calling "messy prayers"—as they tend to the fireplace of spirituality within their home (fig. 4.1). Specifically, this looks like praying together daily and reading the Bible together weekly. So, inside spiritually vibrant homes people are relating to God together, but how exactly do they go about doing that?

When we pull back the curtains and look inside those spiritually vibrant homes that are relating to God together, what do we learn?

Finding 1. Households that relate to God together tend to do a lot together. There is a strong correlation between doing spiritual practices together and doing lots of other household activities together. Figure 4.2 illustrates this strong correlation. Along the bottom of the graph is a list of everyday activities. Notice that households that "shared prayer or Bible reading" did more of everything together when compared with households that had "no shared prayer or Bible reading."

The findings don't point to causation (If you pray together, does that mean you will have more fun together? Or vice versa?),

FIGURE 4.1

ALL HOUSEHOLD ACTIVITIES, BY PARTICIPATION IN SHARED PRAYER AND BIBLE-READING

PERCENT OF RESPONDENTS IN EACH HOUSEHOLD FAITH ENGAGEMENT CATEGORY WHO SAY THEY DO THESE ACTIVITIES TOGETHER WITH THEIR HOUSEMATES

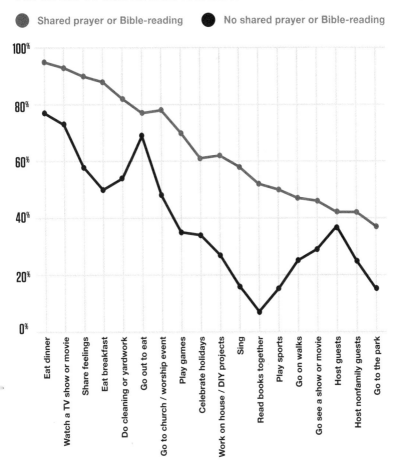

● Shared prayer or Bible-reading   ● No shared prayer or Bible-reading

n=2,347 US practicing Christian adults and teens, April 5–11, 2018.
Question specified these as activities shared at least monthly with
"the people who live with you."

FIGURE 4.2

but they do show that "good fun, good work, and good faith" go hand in hand.[6] This dispels the myth that families who pray and read the Bible together are somehow stiff and overly serious families who never have any fun. Instead, it reveals spiritually vibrant homes as fun and engaged households that value "being present, interested and engaged in the lives" of each other.[7] Perhaps it shouldn't surprise us that there is a correlation between regularly tending to the fireplace of spiritual growth and regularly doing lots of things together.

> **1.** Which of the eighteen activities on the bottom of figure 4.2 do you most often do together with your household?
>
> **2.** How often do those in your household share prayer or Bible reading together?
>
> **3.** How comfortable are those in your household with praying together?

Finding 2. Having an extended household helps. It turns out there is a correlation between how extended a household is and the spiritual vibrancy of that household. As the researchers concluded, "Christians need outside influences for robust faith formation."[8] For children in particular there is something important about relating to adult Christians who aren't your parents. Related research suggests that if kids have relationships with five different

Christian adults, they are more likely to stick with their faith into adulthood.[9]

Why are these additional influences so important? Adults who did not have the Christian faith nurtured in their own family of origin could have a harder time establishing spiritual practices such as prayer and Bible reading, so having additional Christian voices can help tremendously. In other words, the more people we have tending the fire of spiritual practices, the more likely that fire is going to grow and thrive rather than sputter and die. I can testify personally to the ways that my mom's prayers, for example, have strengthened the prayer fire in our household since she's moved in. We are also a stronger household because of the presence of members of our extended household, Cypress and Bosede and the Mackys. These other Christian voices have helped tend to and build up the messy fireplace of our household's prayer life and word life.

1. Refer back to your household map from chapter two. How do the various members of your household affect the overall spiritual vibrancy of your household?

2. Who are a few Christians you would like to have more connected to your household?

3. Think about some of the other people whose extended households you are a part of. How could you affect the overall spiritual vibrancy of their household?

Finding 3. Relating to God together can prepare a household for tough times. Many Christians can testify to the ways their faith has helped them weather a difficult storm. (It helps to have a roaring fire when the weather turns cold and windy.) But the research points to an additional benefit to having a household prayer life and word life. The data shows a correlation between sharing spiritual habits in the home and having each other's backs when life gets difficult.

Three-quarters (76 percent) of those whose households participate in prayer and reading the Bible together recall having a housemate who walked alongside them through a crisis. Only 56 percent of those who do not have a common prayer life or word life recall the same. According to the researchers, this 20 percent difference is statistically significant and meaningful. It is possible that, as the researchers suggest, "Establishing rituals of worship together could build an intimacy that enables relationships to be more supportive in times of need."[10] The data suggests this. There is something deeply bonding about tending to the messy fire of spiritual practices together. It not only warms up our own faith but strengthens the bonds between all those who are gathered together around the fire.

As a pastor I have been inside many homes during times of crisis. I have noticed there that households who already share a prayer life seem to step into the stream of urgent, emotional, mysterious, messy prayer that crisis calls for more readily than households who are triggered by the crisis to pray together for the first time. The habit that is established in normal times comes in handy in times of crisis.

> **1.** Describe a time you had someone in your own core or extended household walk alongside you through a crisis.
>
> **2.** Describe a time your prayer life or word life helped you weather a storm in life.
>
> **3.** Are you in anyone's extended household who is currently weathering a storm? How could you walk alongside them?

Finding 4. The presence of children increases spiritual habits. Simply put, households with children in them have more spiritual conversations, pray more, and read the Bible more, as figure 4.3 clearly shows. Whether this is due to the natural curiosity and spiritual hunger in children (children are quite captivated by a fire in a fireplace, aren't they?) or due to parents' desire to instill the Christian faith remains to be seen. While causation isn't clear, correlation is. Undoubtedly my own children have had this effect on my household—including Victor spurring me on to more robust prayers while tucking him in at night!

SPIRITUAL ACTIVITIES AND THE EFFECT OF MINORS

PERCENT OF RESPONDENTS IN EACH HOUSEHOLD TYPE WHO SAY THEY DO THESE ACTIVITIES TOGETHER WITH THEIR HOUSEMATES

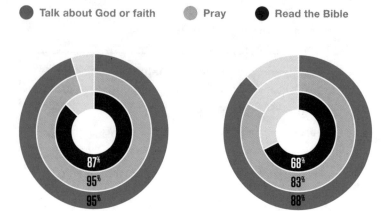

● Talk about God or faith   ● Pray   ● Read the Bible

87%
95%
95%

Households with minors

68%
83%
88%

Households without minors

n=2,347 US practicing Christian adults and teens, April 5–11, 2018. Question specified these as activities shared with "the people who live with you."

FIGURE 4.3

> **1.** If you have children in your own household, how have they affected your household's prayer life or word life?
>
> **2.** If you are an extended household member of a household with children (a grandparent, for example), how have these children had an effect on the overall household's spiritual habits?
>
> **3.** What resources (like a children's Bible or memorized sing-song prayers, for example) do you already have that can help you nurture the prayer life or word life of these children?

Finding 5. Leadership matters. Usually, prayer and handling the Bible don't just happen within a household. The research reveals evidence of spiritual coaching within vibrant households—it is important that someone initiates or encourages a household's spiritual habits. Someone needs to go to the fireplace and call out, "Hey, should we start a fire?"

The good news is that spiritual coaches don't have to be fire experts (experienced prayer leaders or mature students of the Bible); they just need to initiate. A spiritual coach can simply say, "Hey, should someone say a prayer now?" That simple act of initiation can be a difference maker. This, in essence, is what Victor did for me when he asked me to pray out loud. Victor's innocent nighttime request was actually a moment of spiritual coaching.

While anyone can fulfill this simple but important role, some definite trends emerged about who tends to take the initiative, and who doesn't, as you can see in figure 4.4.

Generally speaking, moms and grandparents are quite often the ones initiating spiritual practices in the home. Why is this? Are they quicker to initiate spiritual habits? Do moms tend to be within the household more often? Perhaps grandparents have the time and perspective that give them ease in initiating spiritual practices? As you can see, spouses and roommates tend to struggle to initiate time in prayer or handling the Bible. And dads, in the words of the researchers, tend to "lag behind mothers in spiritual coaching."[11] Perhaps I'm not alone in lagging behind my wife at bedtime prayers?

1. Who most often initiates a moment of prayer or time in the Bible in your household?

2. What is your own comfort level in initiating a moment of prayer or time in the Bible? (Does the news that the simple act of initiating can be a real difference maker affect your comfort level?)

3. How free do you feel to initiate a spiritual moment in any of the households you are an extended member of?

Spending time peering behind the curtains of spiritually vibrant homes can teach us a lot. Not only do we learn how

COMMON SPIRITUAL COACHES
IN ALL HOUSEHOLDS

HOW DO THE PEOPLE IN YOUR HOUSEHOLD OR EXTENDED HOUSEHOLD
TALK TO YOU ABOUT THEIR FAITH?

	Teaches me about the Bible	Talks with me about God's forgiveness	Sets an example	Teaches me about traditions	Encourages me to go to church	Encourages me in other ways
1	Grandparent 55%	Grandparent 56%	Grandparent 67%	Grandparent 67%	Grandparent 65%	Grandparent 62%
2	Mother 49%	Mother 52%	Mother 58%	Mother 53%	Mother 61%	Spouse 60%
3	Father 44%	Father 43%	Father 56%	Father 48%	Father 51%	Mother 57%
4	Spouse 34%	Spouse 39%	Spouse 48%	Stepparent 32%	Spouse 44%	Father 53%
5	Roommate 29%	Friend 34%	Stepparent 44%	In-laws 30%	Stepparent 41%	Friend 48%
6	Stepparent 26%	Roommate 29%	Friend 38%	Friend 26%	In-laws 41%	Stepparent 47%
7	Friend 23%	Stepparent 29%	In-laws 36%	Spouse 25%	Friend 32%	In-laws 44%
8	Unmarried partner 21%	In-laws 28%	Other relative 31%	Other non-relative 22%	Unmarried partner 29%	Unmarried partner 44%
9	Other non-relative 21%	Unmarried partner 25%	Unmarried partner 30%	Roommate 21%	Roommate 28%	Other relative 41%
10	Other relative 20%	Other relative 25%	Sibling 28%	Other relative 20%	Other relative 27%	Sibling 32%
11	In-laws 18%	Other non-relative 24%	Roommate 27%	Sibling 17%	Sibling 24%	Other non-relative 31%
12	Sibling 14%	Sibling 19%	Other non-relative 23%	Unmarried partner 16%	Other non-relative 20%	Grandchild 31%
13	Child 8%	Child 14%	Grandchild 15%	Child 7%	Child 13%	Roommate 30%
14	Grandchild 7%	Grandchild 11%	Child 13%	Grandchild 6%	Grandchild 12%	Child 26%

n=2,347 US practicing Christian adults and teens, April 5–11, 2018. Respondents were only shown relationship types they live with or who visit them regularly in their home, not including children under age 18.

FIGURE 4.4

important it is to be engaged in the spiritual habits of prayer and Bible reading, but we also glean these other findings of how spiritually vibrant homes pray and handle the Bible.

But how exactly can we put this "wisdom, understanding, and knowledge" to use in building our own households and filling their rooms with "all precious and pleasant riches" as Proverbs 24:3-4 so beautifully invited us back in chapter three?

HOW CAN I HELP MY HOUSEHOLD RELATE TO GOD?

There is a stressful temptation I would like us to avoid at this point. The temptation is to create a picture of the ideal household and try, duty bound, to replicate that picture within our own household. We care about our household and desire for it to be as spiritually vibrant as possible, so it is mighty tempting therefore to try to force our household to fit some ideal.

History is littered with books that promise the exact recipe for creating and shaping the ideal household: for example, *The Domostroi: Rules for Russian Households in the Time of Ivan the Terrible* (a sixteenth-century guide to good Christian household management) and *Mrs. Beeton's Book of Household Management* (published in 1861 and full of advice on "cooking, cleaning, childrearing, entertaining, and more"). If you were to flip through a few books like these, as I have, I wonder if you would have the same reaction I did: complete exhaustion. There's something so compelling and yet so heavy and stressful and reductionistic about extensive lists and exacting ideals.

I'd like to avoid this stressful temptation. I believe it is possible to ask the practical question, How can I help my household relate to God? while avoiding the trap of duty-bound list checking. Perhaps the image of a fireplace can be helpful again. If we are used to a furnace, we have thermostat expectations. I can set the dial to an exact degree and the furnace will get the house to that desired temperature within a few minutes. Furnaces are wonderful in this way.

But our spiritual growth (including our growth in relating to God as a household) doesn't work that way. There's no magical thermostat. There's no master furnace in a separate room that will quickly change the spiritual temperature of our household. Spiritual growth is more like a fireplace. It is possible to encourage and nurture a fire, but nothing about it is automatic. Or quick. It takes regular, patient, inglorious attention. At times you have to arrange the kindling; at other times it's more important to add another log on the fire, and sometimes you need to stoke the coals (fig. 4.5).

When it comes to applying spiritual disciplines, we can nurture these shared habits in the same ways we would nurture a fire, both in our households and in the households we are extended members of.

Arrange the kindling. Want to start a fire? There's actually an art to starting a fire. Every Boy Scout and Girl Scout knows you need to start by arranging kindling. You take those few small, thin grasses or branches and try to spark a small fire. Sometimes it takes a few matches to catch, doesn't it? It takes patience, and a little blowing—but not *too much* or you might snuff it out.

Getting a household to start relating to God together is not unlike that process. It is a tender thing to get a household praying, to get a household handling the Bible a little. You can't

The Spiritually Vibrant Home

MESSY PRAYERS	LOUD TABLES	OPEN DOORS
1. Arrange the kindling 2. Add another log 3. Stoke the coals		

FIGURE 4.5

force it. But you can keep at it until the flame catches. Here are some ways you could arrange some spiritual kindling in your own household:

- Spend more time together playing, eating, or simply having fun. Remember, the research shows a correlation between doing *lots* together (including lots of food and fun) and doing spiritual activities together.

- Insert an occasional short prayer into your life (like at bedtime or mealtimes). It could be something short and sweet and genuine. Even a nice memorized prayer (Now I lay me down to sleep . . .) might do the trick.

- Get some words of Scripture up on your walls. Just follow the Moab call (Deuteronomy 6:6-7, 9) quite literally by hanging a note, sign, or piece of artwork that has a Scripture passage on it somewhere in your home or car— even on your doorposts or gate if you want! (In our household we recently started writing a Bible verse on our hall mirror with a dry erase marker. Every now and then I ask one of my kids to choose a new verse and write it on the mirror.)

- Buy a new Bible that has a colorful, attractive cover and leave it lying around the house.

There's a variety of small things you could do to arrange the tender kindling and create some sparks.

Add another log. Want to grow your existing fire? You add another log—not too many at once or you will choke out the fire. And not too big of a log lest you collapse the burning structure underneath and choke out the air flow. Just add another log and let the fire adjust to it, warm it, and spread throughout it. That's how fire grows.

Helping a household grow in its relating to God is not unlike that process. It is a gradual thing to help flames grow higher. Here are some ways you could add another spiritual log to the fire in your household:

- Start inserting short, momentary prayers into your common life. For example, if someone mentions they've had a bad day or are nervous about an upcoming event, just "go live" and say a quick prayer for them on the spot.

- Pray a quick blessing for people who are headed out the door. Blessings can be as brief as "May God bless you and give you what you need for your big day." Simply start with the words "May God . . ." and then finish the sentence.

- Do a daily or weekly Scripture reading during special seasons like Advent, Lent, or a family vacation.

- Use memorized or written prayers together on occasion. Try praying the Lord's Prayer together before a meal—many people already have it memorized! Or read aloud a written prayer from a church bulletin. (I recently discovered *Every Moment Holy*, a wonderful book filled with written prayers for everyday moments.[12] In our first two weeks with the book in our home we used liturgies specifically written for "before a purposeful gathering," "when a family received a new pet," and "for those who are about to consume media." Now, my friends and family are always asking me if I have a liturgy for whatever we're about to do. I think they are half-teasing me, but I don't mind—I pull out the book and look for an appropriate prayer to read!)

- Ask a question at mealtime about the Bible text from the last sermon you all heard together.

- Create a jar filled with "prayer sticks"—simple craft sticks that anyone can write a name on (one stick for grandma, another for grandpa, a stick for that new kid at school, a stick for each of your good friends from high school that are away at different colleges) and keep the sticks in a jar. At meals or bedtime have everyone grab one stick and say a prayer for that person.

Again, adding too much wood (or pieces of wood that are too big) to a fire can choke out the fire. Use your intuition—try adding one right-sized new piece and see what happens.

Stoke the coals. Want to rouse a dormant fire? Usually, that requires stoking the coals—there's heat enough in those coals, they just need to be jostled, brought back out into contact with the air, brought into contact with some other wood.

Sometimes helping restore a household's historical ways of relating to God is that simple, just bring back into play some of the great spiritual practices that have always been there. It is a slightly disturbing but quite rewarding thing to expose dormant embers. And sometimes it actually helps a fire to shake it up a bit, to bring more hot coals into play! Here are some ways you could stoke the spiritual coals in your own household:

- Purposefully extend your household. Bring more Christians into your household by inviting people over for a meal or event.

- Host a prayer event or regular Bible study in your home. Bringing the *sacred* into your own *secular* home can fight against the temptation of the sacred-secular split.

- Take your entire household to a spiritually themed event. Many retreat centers offer retreats that all different household types could engage in together.

- Together, volunteer for an event that will involve moments of prayer and time in the Bible. For example, you could all volunteer at your church's Vacation Bible School or go on a short-term mission trip together.

- Host a movie night and watch a movie that is faith-based.

- Go multigenerational. Whether inviting people to move in or to simply come over, you can take steps to insure that children and grandparent-types (whether they are related to you or not) are more a part of your household.

In these and other ways you could purposefully stoke the coals of the fire within your household, bringing new hot coals out into the open.

CAN I REALLY HAVE MESSY PRAYERS IN MY HOUSEHOLD?

As I experienced through Victor's simple persistence, it doesn't take much to see your prayer life and word life alter as a household. Fires just need fuel, oxygen, and heat. Get those different pieces together and create a couple of sparks and you never know just what might happen.

If applying spiritual disciplines together in your household seems like a daunting new endeavor, remember that this household habit is really quite old and is how God intended households to function from the very beginning. Your household is made for this.

Not only is your household made for messy prayers, remember that Jesus came to help us be in a living relationship with God. As we take practical steps to nurture messy prayer in our homes, it can be encouraging to remember that Jesus worked (and still works) to help us with this task.

Jesus came to earth so that we could be in an intimate relationship with God. As he put it, "I am the way, and the truth, and the life. No one comes to the Father except through me" (John 14:6). Through Jesus' sacrifice on the cross, a way was made for us and all those in our household to come to the Father and pursue a living relationship with him.

Jesus also sent us the gift of the Holy Spirit so that we could grow that living relationship with God. The apostle Paul described the relational effects of the Spirit in Romans: "God's love has been poured into our hearts through the Holy Spirit who has been given to us" (Romans 5:5). The Spirit pours God's love into our hearts, growing our relationship with him.

Jesus also modeled a living relationship with the Father. As Brenda Colijn put it in her survey on the family in the Bible, "Jesus reveals God as his Father in a special sense and addresses God as 'Abba,' an Aramaic term of intimate family relationship, similar to 'Papa.' Jesus invited his disciples to have the same intimacy with God that he had—and that only he could bestow."[13]

Jesus' model of relating to God as Father should not be taken lightly. His teachings on the fatherhood of God were unparalleled in his time, and by addressing God as *Abba*, he introduced humanity to a new way of relating to God.[14]

Not only is your household made to relate to God together, but Jesus came to help us do just that. When we seek to grow and nurture our household's relationship with God, we are simply joining Jesus in what he is working toward within us every day.

In other words, the wood is dry and there's plenty of oxygen and heat. God wants us to relate to him. And the more we do, the more spiritually vibrant our home will become.

HOW CAN I PURSUE FOCUSED GROWTH IN THIS AREA?

While spiritual coaches need only to initiate to make a difference, it obviously can be helpful to become more equipped over time as a spiritual coach. If helping your household relate to God is something you want to spend some significant time growing in, here are a few resources inspired by this latest research to help you pursue personal growth in this area. Even if you are new to prayer and reading the Bible yourself, you can still invite your household to grow in these shared spiritual disciplines right along with you.

- "Building a Vibrant Household." This course explores spiritually vibrant households and the three characteristics revealed by research that any household can nurture. It will equip you to evaluate your own household's vibrancy and to take next steps in building a more vibrant household. This course can be found at www.lhm.org/households.

- "Helping Your Child Have a Relationship with God." Parents have high hopes for their children's faith, but they don't always know how to get them there. This booklet helps parents nurture their child's relationship with God by exploring how to partner with God using two practical rhythms that will help their child learn how to pray to God and understand his Word. This booklet can be found at www.lhm.org/households.

- "Learning to Pray." This booklet is geared toward preschool to third-grade children. It is written in rhyme to teach and encourage children (and parents) to spend time with God in prayer. This booklet can be found at www.lhm.org/households.

- "The Bible Tells Me So." This kids' booklet provides several key Bible verses that speak to God's love, his mercy, his forgiveness, and his words of guidance. It reminds children to look to the Bible to learn how to live their lives for God. This booklet can be found at www.lhm.org/households.

5

LOUD TABLES

HELPING OUR HOUSEHOLDS HAVE SPIRITUAL CONVERSATIONS

These words that I command you today shall be on your heart. You shall teach them diligently to your children, and shall talk of them when you sit in your house, and when you walk by the way, and when you lie down, and when you rise.

DEUTERONOMY 6:6-7

I was a college student on summer break when my dad asked me this seemingly benign question: "Where do you want to go for dinner?" We were in his car, driving out of his apartment complex one night to get dinner. I had been staying with my dad in Memphis for a couple of weeks during my break from school. During the day he went to work and I stayed back at his place reading books and relaxing. At night he'd come home and we would usually head out to dinner somewhere.

This night my dad was simply asking, as we pulled out of the parking lot, where we should go. "It's not really important to me," I said with a shrug.

Maybe it was something in my nonchalant tone. Maybe it was how quiet I had been during the trip. For whatever reason, my dad looked over at me and asked, with real, genuine interest, "What is important to you?"

It was clear my dad was inviting me into a deep conversation, a spiritual conversation, even. He was inviting me to open up about myself and talk with him about what was going on inside me and in my life.

At the time there was *a lot* going on inside me and in my life. I was leading Bible studies on campus. I was learning how to lead worship. I had started spending weeks at a time volunteering in the inner city. I was even contemplating a ministry internship after graduating from college. There was *so much* going on inside me and in my life, and even though we were still driving, looking for a place to sit down and eat dinner, my dad was in essence pulling out a chair and inviting me to sit with him in a conversation.

My dad kept driving, and his question and invitation hung in the air between us. I looked out the window to my right. *Would I accept the invitation? Would I let my dad in on everything? Would we have a spiritual conversation right there in the car?*

Dad and I had never been big into deep conversations. Our household growing up wasn't necessarily a place where we talked a lot. Our dinner table was more on the quiet side. We moved often as a family, and these constant moves gave each of us, I suppose, a fair amount of chaos to deal with. As for myself, I developed my nomadic ways (quick to make friends at my new school, quick to forget them), which left me seeking solitude when I was at home. While I was growing up, Dad was at work a lot. I was happy escaping into my books. We didn't have a lot of conversations. Early in my high school years, my father had moved to a different state, which left us even less time at the table and fewer opportunities to talk.

Which is why my dad's question was such a surprising thing. "What is important to you?" By his tone I could tell he was really interested. In college I had begun to have lots of deep, spiritual conversations—and I loved them. But here's the thing, I had never had a spiritual conversation like that *with my dad*. It felt new and scary and vulnerable. "What is important to you?" Do I sit down at the chair my dad had pulled out for me, engaging in a spiritual conversation?

I didn't even look at my dad. I shrugged and said, "I don't know."

For whatever reason (or reasons) I did not enter into a conversation that day. We chatted about inconsequential things over ribs that night but had no real conversation. But even in my reticence that night I couldn't deny that I was pretty sure engaging in a spiritual conversation with my dad should be a normal thing.

I know that my own reticence to enter into a conversation with my father has very personal reasons: my introversion, years of not talking deeply together, my unfortunate self-protective habits. There are plenty of Don-specific reasons that a spiritual conversation with my dad felt like kryptonite to me. But it is also important to recognize that we live in a specific time and age when spiritual conversations, in general, aren't doing too well.

As I explored in *The Reluctant Witness: Discovering the Delight of Spiritual Conversations*, the latest research tells us we are having fewer spiritual conversations.[1] In fact, LHM and Barna found that a full three-quarters of all self-identified Christians have *fewer than ten* spiritual conversations a year. This includes a conversation with anyone about faith: a discussion at a Bible study counts, a conversation with your spouse counts, discussing the recent sermon counts. Most Christians are having less than one of those conversations per month. Most Christians are, as the researchers concluded, "reluctant conversationalists." Our tables are pretty quiet.

The research delved into various reasons *why* the cat has got our tongues when it comes to spiritual conversations (for example, secularism, relativism, pluralism, and the fear of offense), but sociologist and psychologist Sherry Turkle argues in *Reclaiming Conversation* that our digital age and new digital means of communication are significant factors in our exodus from any sort of deeper conversation, whether spiritual or otherwise. She describes the net effect of technology-mediated communication: "It all adds up to a flight from conversation—at least from conversation that is open-ended and spontaneous, conversation in which we play with ideas, in which we allow ourselves to be fully present and vulnerable."[2]

Turkle laments this flight from conversation because she is convinced that "face-to-face conversation is the most human—and humanizing—thing we do."[3] In other words, loud tables are important. Theologian Wesley Hill agrees but argues in his book *Spiritual Friendship* that we are seeing less and less deep conversations because a particular "myth of freedom" makes us shy away from deeper relationships. Wesley explains why friendship has seemingly gone out of style: "It's . . . the myth that the less encumbered and entangled I am, or the less accountable and anchored I am to a particular relationship, the better able I am to find my truest self and secure real happiness. . . . If your deepest fulfillment is found in personal autonomy, then friendship . . . is more of a liability than an asset."[4]

Just as I had a sneaking suspicion that this silence between my dad and me wasn't right, many of us sense this reluctance toward conversations isn't how God designed us to live. It turns out our sense is right. Our household tables are meant to be on the louder side.

ARE WE MEANT TO RELATE TO EACH OTHER IN A HOUSEHOLD?

It turns out that God designed us to be in relationship with each other. Throughout the Bible, God makes it clear that his people are intended to relate to each other in spiritual conversations *even in their own households*.

Consider that Plains of Moab moment again. Right at that threshold moment when God clarifies that households are to relate to him, he is also quite clear that this naturally will involve spiritual conversations. Deuteronomy 6 says, "These words that I command you today shall be on your heart. You shall teach them diligently to your children, and shall talk of them when you sit in your house, and when you walk by the way, and when you lie down, and when you rise" (Deuteronomy 6:6-7).

God intends us to talk with each other about his words and our relationship with him when we're sitting at home, when we're walking along the road, when we lie down at night, when we get up in the morning. By my math, that's a lot of spiritual conversations! In our houses, in the minivan, over breakfast, and at bedtime. We are called by God to be a people of spiritual conversations. This call to relational intimacy and regular spiritual conversations didn't change when Jesus came. If anything, it intensified.

Jesus had an intimate, ongoing relationship with God the Father, and he related to his own disciples in the same way. As Jesus put it, "As the Father has loved me, so have I loved you"

(John 15:9). And not only did Jesus invite his disciples into an intimate, loving relationship with him, but he also called them to relate to each other in the same way: "A new commandment I give to you, that you love one another: just as I have loved you, you also are to love one another. By this all people will know that you are my disciples, if you have love for one another" (John 13:34-35).

And the disciples did just that. As Hill notes, "The disciples weren't orphans or pariahs as they hiked along with Jesus in Galilee and, ultimately, joined him on his final journey to Jerusalem. They were adoptees—given, by Jesus, an entirely new set of parents, siblings, and cousins, brought into a new circle of kin and spiritual relations. In a sense, they were made friends of one another."[5]

Ultimately the good news of Jesus is redemptive news. Jesus came to do his repair work of reconnecting us to God, to each other, and to the wider world around us. This clearly had radical effects on people's relationships with each other. As Hill keenly observes, "There is something happening, the Gospels suggest, that compels us to pursue friendships, rather than just leaving them available, as something we can take or leave. 'The Kingdom of God is at hand,' Jesus announces, and nothing—including our human relationships—can ever be the same."[6]

Throughout the Bible God is clear that we are invited to have intimate relationships with each other, within our households and without, and this inevitably and beautifully includes having spiritual conversations.

WHICH IS BETTER: A CONTROLLABLE TELEVISION OR A LOUD TABLE?

There is something simultaneously exciting and scary about this. The flight from conversations that is so common today may not be too biblical, but it is safe. Conversations (especially deeper, spiritual conversations) are intimate, vulnerable things. In this fallen world that's a hard thing to choose.

There is something safe about covering up. There is something safe about surface conversations. There is something easy about just shrugging and saying, "I don't know," when your dad asks you what's important to you. You aren't exposed; you aren't open to rejection; you aren't finding yourself in the less predictable waters of Turkle's face-to-face, "open-ended and spontaneous" conversations.

You can see the appeal, I'm sure. Avoiding spiritual conversations is safe and relieves us of the inherent vulnerability and intimacy that comes with relating to each other on a deeper level. The difference between this safe model and the biblical model, it seems to me, is similar to the difference between a television and a table.

With a television (or any screen, for that matter), you get to taste all sorts of human interactions: funny ones, deep ones, adventurous ones, tragic ones. But you are in control the whole time. Want to laugh? Turn on a sitcom and join the show's warm family as they bumble and joke their way through an episode. Want to cry? Just flip over to that romance movie and find yourself getting lost in the twists and turns of love and flirting and affection and temptation. Want to get your heart racing? There's a great new action series streaming this month. Feeling thoughtful? You can always try one of those documentaries or an existentially intense foreign film.

Here's the great thing about television: you get to experience humanity and yet remain in control the whole time. You know what you are getting when you turn on the show. You get to control the volume. And you can turn it off whenever you want. You get any human experience you want with none of the pesky intimacy and vulnerability.

The biblical model is much more spontaneous and potentially intimate. Kind of like gathering around a table. When you gather around a table with others, what do you see? Each other. And what will you experience? Well, that depends, doesn't it? It will definitely be a human experience, but of what sort? That's the thing about conversation—it is live. You never know whether a conversation will lead to laughter or tears or a racing heart or deep thoughts.

And whenever you gather around the table, you *yourself* are part of what's going on. Watching a television allows you to be aloof, not involved personally. But when you gather at a table with others, you yourself are present to be loved or cajoled or ignored or asked questions. *What if Dad thinks it's weird that I'm considering this ministry internship?* And in this fallen world that is a scary prospect.

But even though gathering around a table for a meal isn't safe or controllable, I have to admit there's something so captivating and *alive* about sitting in a circle with others. This is perhaps what makes Jen Pollock Michel conclude that at the end of the day our tables are our most important piece of furniture.[7] There is something electric and warm and inviting about gathering with others around a table and entering right into a conversation. Especially a spiritual conversation.

FIGURE 5.1

While the television and the flight from conversations have their appeal, the Bible is clear that we are meant to relate to each other in spiritual conversations. It's to be the table, not the television. And the research supports this.

WHAT CAN WE LEARN ABOUT RELATING TO EACH OTHER FROM SPIRITUALLY VIBRANT HOMES?

The second of three household habits that corresponds with greater spiritual vibrancy within the household is "engaging in spiritual conversations"—what we're calling the loud table (fig. 5.1). Specifically, the loud table includes talking about God and faith weekly. So, inside spiritually vibrant homes people are relating to each other, but how exactly do they go about doing that?

When we pull back the curtains and look inside those spiritually vibrant homes that are talking with each other about God and faith, what do we learn?

Finding 1. Households that engage in spiritual conversations tend to do a lot together. The correlation we noticed in chapter four between households that do lots of things together and those that share spiritual habits together is similar for households that engage in spiritual conversations, as you can see in figure 5.2

Along the bottom of the graph is a list of everyday activities. Notice that households that engaged in spiritual conversations did more of everything together when compared with households that had "no spiritual conversations." We can't

ALL HOUSEHOLD ACTIVITIES, BY PARTICIPATION IN SPIRITUAL CONVERSATIONS

PERCENT OF RESPONDENTS IN EACH HOUSEHOLD FAITH ENGAGEMENT CATEGORY WHO SAY THEY DO THESE ACTIVITIES TOGETHER WITH THEIR HOUSEMATES

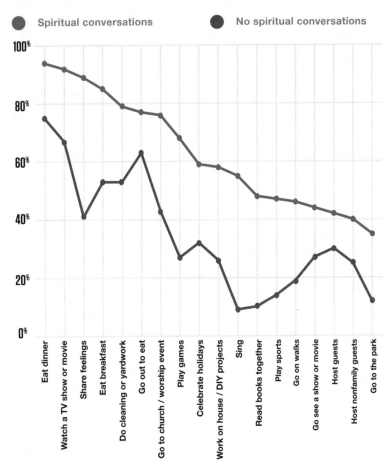

● Spiritual conversations ● No spiritual conversations

n=2,347 US practicing Christian adults and teens, April 5–11, 2018. Question specified these as activities shared at least monthly with "the people who live with you."

FIGURE 5.2

exactly determine causation, but I can say from my own experience that spending time together having fun, eating food, and doing chores primes the pump for deeper interactions. Through everyday activities trust is built. And trust is an important prerequisite for spiritual conversations.

Recall that the most common terms used to describe the atmosphere in a spiritually vibrant home were words like *comfortable*, *loving*, *safe*, *peaceful*, *casual*, *joyful*, and *playful*. A variety of common activities helps create this kind of atmosphere in a home, which is key to shaping an environment that is friendly to spiritual conversations. As the researchers noted, "Many members of households and extended households engage with one another in a number of dimensions, a diversity of interactions that can have a positive correlation with the overall atmosphere and spiritual nourishment of a home."[8]

1. How often would you say members of your household talk about God and their faith?

2. Which of the members of your household would you consider "eager conversationalists"? Who are more "reluctant conversationalists"?

3. Think back to the last spiritual conversation your household engaged in. What were the circumstances for that conversation? Where and when did it take place?

REGULAR AT-HOME ROUTINES SHARED WITH ALL HOUSEHOLD MEMBERS

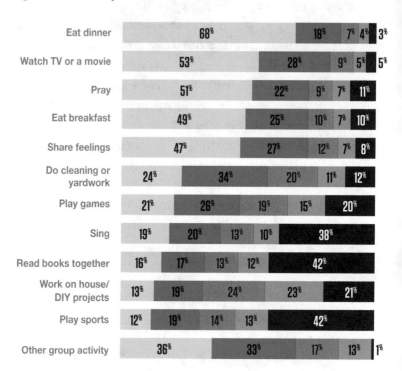

- Every day or two
- At least weekly
- Less than weekly but at least once a month
- Less than once a month
- We don't do this

Activity	Every day or two	At least weekly	Less than weekly but at least once a month	Less than once a month	We don't do this
Eat dinner	68%	18%	7%	4%	3%
Watch TV or a movie	53%	28%	9%	5%	5%
Pray	51%	22%	9%	7%	11%
Eat breakfast	49%	25%	10%	7%	10%
Share feelings	47%	27%	12%	7%	8%
Do cleaning or yardwork	24%	34%	20%	11%	12%
Play games	21%	26%	19%	15%	20%
Sing	19%	20%	13%	10%	38%
Read books together	16%	17%	13%	12%	42%
Work on house/DIY projects	13%	19%	24%	23%	21%
Play sports	12%	19%	14%	13%	42%
Other group activity	36%	33%	17%	13%	1%

n=2,347 US practicing Christian adults and teens, April 5–11, 2018. Question specified these as activities shared with "the people who live with you."

FIGURE 5.3

Finding 2. Many conversations happen around a table.
If household members are all together, they are typically gathered around the table. The research found that eating dinner together (every day or every other day) is the most common group activity in practicing Christian homes; as you can see in figure 5.3 eating together even beats out watching television together. Half of these same homes also include shared breakfast in their routines, which, when combined with dinners, makes mealtime a significant feature of household togetherness.

While conversations can obviously happen while gathered around a television or doing yardwork, gathering around a meal is much more conducive to conversations of many kinds, especially deeper conversations, which tend to take more time to unfold. As the researchers noted, this table togetherness can happen around food in a variety of places, "Beyond the home, food is also the impetus for togetherness. Three-quarters of respondents (76%), and couples in particular (90%), go out to eat at least once a month as a group."[9] Whether inside the home or not, gathering around a table for food creates space for conversations, especially if screens are not present.

> **1.** How often does your core household eat together? Does your extended household ever get together for a meal?

2. If you are a member of someone else's extended household, how often are you eating with that household?

3. How present are screens when you do eat together, whether at home or at a restaurant?

Finding 3. Spiritual friendships are important. One of the clear patterns that emerged in the research was that while there are a number of relationships that "shape and uplift practicing Christians," those relationships that are more regular, intimate, and one-on-one are the most dependable source of support and growth. As the researchers concluded, "Our most frequent companions and our most dependable ones tend to be the same."[10]

For those who are married, their spouse tends to be a significant spiritual friend. Spouses not only share everyday, mundane activities like watching television, doing chores, and running a household, but they also confide in one another, confront one another, and pray together.[11] It should be noted that this close spiritual friendship is complicated when children are a part of the household, but "spouses may begin to lean on and enjoy each other again once they have finished their child-rearing years."[12]

While marriages are a source of significant friendship, the researchers found that other close friendships are nearly as crucial in vibrant households, and the importance of fostering

HOUSEHOLDS AND THEIR CLOSEST FRIENDS

DO YOU HAVE ANY PEOPLE IN YOUR LIFE WHO ARE SO CLOSE THAT
THEY FEEL LIKE FAMILY?

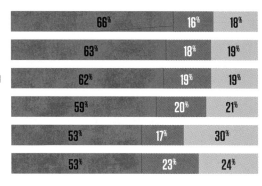

● One or two ● More than two ● None

Household	One or two	More than two	None
Single-parent household	66%	16%	18%
Roommate household	63%	18%	19%
Nuclear family household	62%	19%	19%
Multigenerational household	59%	20%	21%
Couple household	53%	17%	30%
Other households	53%	23%	24%

n=2,347 US practicing Christian adults and teens, April 5–11, 2018.

FIGURE 5.4

intimacy with those who are a part of the extended household "cannot be overstated."[13]

We need multiple spiritual friends. These are people who feel like family that we communicate with on a regular basis and engage in deep conversation with. Figure 5.4 shows how common these types of close friends are in practicing Christian homes, no matter what household type. Engaging in spiritual conversations "about God's forgiveness, the Bible, traditions or commending church attendance" correlates with stronger spiritual vibrancy.[14]

> **1.** How many people in your extended household are so close they feel like family? One or two? More than two? None?
>
> **2.** Who is your most common conversation partner for talking about God and faith?
>
> **3.** Who in your household (core or extended) would you most like to engage with in more spiritual conversations?

Finding 4. Spiritual coaching helps. Researchers noticed the presence of "intentional . . . even pastoral" spiritual coaching, including spiritual instruction and encouragement, setting an example, encouraging church attendance, and sharing about God's forgiveness, the Bible, and traditions.[15] But while there's great variation, much of this coaching happened, understandably, through spiritual conversations.

HOUSEHOLD TYPES AND FAITH ENGAGEMENT AT HOME

PERCENT OF RESPONDENTS IN EACH HOUSEHOLD TYPE WHO SAY THEY DO THESE ACTIVITIES TOGETHER WITH THEIR HOUSEMATES

● Talk about God or faith   ● Pray   ● Read the Bible

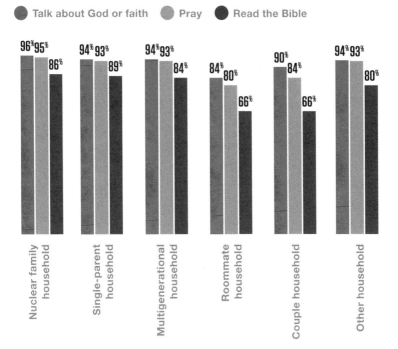

Nuclear family household: 96% 95% 86%
Single-parent household: 94% 93% 89%
Multigenerational household: 94% 93% 84%
Roommate household: 84% 80% 66%
Couple household: 90% 84% 66%
Other household: 94% 93% 80%

n=2,347 US practicing Christian adults and teens, April 5–11, 2018. Question specified these as activities shared with "the people who live with you."

FIGURE 5.5

Mothers and grandparents are quite regular spiritual coaches. In fact, as the researchers noted, "Grandparents hardly ever participate in a household without trying to lead or interact on a spiritual level."[16] Often all the coaching that is needed is initiating, being willing to try to start a spiritual conversation—like asking your quiet son, "What is important to you?" In fact, the data tells us spiritual conversations are the most common form of faith engagement in most households. This is true no matter what household type we are talking about as seen in figure 5.5. This may come as encouraging news for those hoping to start spiritual conversations in their home.

1. Think about the person in your household who most often initiates spiritual conversations. How do they generally initiate those conversations?

2. Reflecting back on past spiritual conversations, do you notice any trends in what is most helpful in initiating a spiritual conversation in your home?

3. If you are a member of someone else's extended household, how free do you feel to initiate deeper conversations there?

Finding 5. Some people struggle more with conversations. The research shows us that not everyone has the same level of ease in initiating or engaging in spiritual conversations.

Consider, for example, what the research findings revealed about adult nuclear families. In those households where adult children are living with their parents, there is a much lower level of group activities of all kinds—including spiritual conversations.

Or consider what the research revealed about different generations. While millennials (1984–1998) are most likely to engage in conversations about sensitive subjects, boomers (1946–1964) more than any other generation say they discuss more delicate subjects with no one.[17] It would appear that some generations are, generally speaking, more or less comfortable in engaging in spiritual conversations.

A third significant finding has to do with dads. While practicing Christians are clear that they look to their dads as examples, it is sobering to read that the data led the researchers to conclude that

> practicing Christians in this study don't seem to share much quality time with their fathers, compared to other immediate and sometimes extended household ties. Accordingly, fathers seem to be disconnected when it comes to the actual feelings and goings-on of their housemates, namely their spouses and children. These trends become especially pronounced—and worrisome—when tracking teenagers' responses.[18]

Although the biblical narrative suggests that both parents are to bring up children in the fear of the Lord, the reality revealed in this study is that regardless of a family's theology or philosophy about mothers' and fathers' respective roles, mothers consistently exceed fathers in instilling children with the values and discipline of the faith. Moms pray more with their children and talk about God and the Bible and questions of faith more with their children as you can see in figure 5.6.[19] My own struggles praying with Victor at night (especially compared to Wendy) would be an apt example of this.

Of course, you don't have to be in an adult nuclear home or be a boomer or a dad to struggle with spiritual conversations, but given how important spiritual conversations are for a vibrant household, those who typically struggle more in engaging in them need to pay special attention to this important household habit.

1. Are there any members of your household who you'd say struggle with deeper spiritual conversations? Where do you think their struggles come from?

2. Reflecting on your own spiritual conversations, what has helped you become more willing to engage in or initiate spiritual conversations?

3. Who do you know (whether in your household or not) who is strong in initiating and engaging in spiritual conversations? What do you notice about how they approach spiritual conversations?

WHO ARE YOU MOST LIKELY TO TALK WITH ABOUT . . .?

	Questions about faith	Something that bothers you	Sex	The Bible	Politics
1	Spouse 73%	Spouse 79%	Spouse 74%	Spouse 71%	Spouse 67%
2	Mother 59%	Unmarried partner 68%	Unmarried partner 68%	Unmarried partner 62%	Unmarried partner 55%
3	Unmarried partner 55%	Mother 60%	Friend 39%	Mother 61%	Father 51%
4	Grandparent 55%	Friend 59%	Roommate 26%	Grandparent 60%	Mother 42%
5	Roommate 50%	Sibling 47%	Mother 24%	Father 51%	Roommate 40%
6	Father 49%	Roommate 46%	Father 19%	Friend 45%	Friend 38%
7	Friend 47%	Grandparent 40%	Stepparent 18%	Roommate 45%	Stepparent 37%
8	Stepparent 33%	Father 39%	Sibling 15%	Child 45%	Grandparent 36%
9	Child 32%	Child 38%	Other non-relative 13%	Stepparent 38%	Sibling 30%
10	Sibling 32%	Stepparent 32%	Grandparent 12%	Sibling 36%	Other non-relative 29%
11	Other relative 28%	Other relative 30%	Other relative 12%	Grandchild 35%	In-laws 29%
12	In-laws 25%	Other non-relative 26%	Child 8%	Other relative 32%	Other relative 26%
13	Other non-relative 24%	In-laws 21%	Grandchild 5%	Other non-relative 29%	Child 25%
14	Grandchild 19%	Grandchild 13%	In-laws 2%	In-laws 28%	Grandchild 13%

n=2,347 US practicing Christian adults and teens, April 5–11, 2018. Respondents were only shown relationship types they live with or who visit them regularly in their home.

FIGURE 5.6

HOW CAN I HELP MY HOUSEHOLD
HAVE SPIRITUAL CONVERSATIONS?

Just as we did when looking at applying spiritual disciplines, it is important for us to avoid the stressful temptation of trying to force our households to fit some ideal when it comes to our conversations. I believe it is possible to ask the question, How can my household relate to each other? while avoiding the trap of duty-bound list checking.

Perhaps the image of the table can be helpful again. If we are used to television, we may have what I'll call remote-control expectations: I can switch to whatever type of human interaction I am interested in with the push of a button. Remote controls are wonderful in this way—we don't even have to get off the couch.

But our conversations (especially our spiritual ones) don't work that way. There's no conversation remote control. There's no cued-up menu of conversation options waiting for us to choose from. No, conversations are a group sport—they implicitly involve conversation partners who can't be controlled like a television. It is possible to pursue or nurture or spark a conversation, but it is rarely helpful to try to force one—especially a deeper spiritual conversation. Again, the image of the meal at a table is helpful. You can invite people to a table, you can invite them to eat, but ultimately you can't force food (even really good food) into someone's mouth! No one would stand for that—even if the food would be good for them. You can't force it.

Conversations have to build, like a meal. You start with lighter fare: a salad, a soup, perhaps some tasty hors d'oeuvres. When the appetite is built, you can then move into the hearty, protein-rich entrée—this is the meat-and-potatoes part of the meal. Many meals simply consist of this entrée. But at times, when the moment is right, you bring out the really rich stuff, the tastiest and most extravagant of all—dessert (fig. 5.7). Not

The Spiritually Vibrant Home

MESSY PRAYERS	LOUD TABLES	OPEN DOORS

1. Start with light fare
2. Provide a steady diet
3. Offer a rich dessert

FIGURE 5.7

everyone will have room for dessert (and it doesn't even have to be that large), but it can be the finest part of the meal.

When it comes to engaging in spiritual conversations, we can invite people to sit down to a conversation in the same way we would invite people to sit down to a meal.

Start with light fare. Want to warm people up to a meal? Start with light fare. These are sometimes referred to as "small plates"—and for a reason. They aren't huge, rich affairs. They are light. They are "bites" as some restaurants refer to them. They are a way of whetting the appetite.

Getting a household to start relating to each other is not unlike these hors d'oeuvres. It is a tender thing to get a household talking with each other, engaging in spiritual conversations— especially if this isn't the normal practice in a household. You can't force it. But you can whet people's appetites for it by engaging in lighter, shorter conversations. Never underestimate the power of chatting to help get people talking. Here are some ways you could whet conversational appetites in your own household:

- Ask a question about a recent shared experience. *What did you think of the movie?*

- Share a story from your day. *You'll never guess what happened to me today . . .*

- If you have a pet, take them on a walk or to a park with other members of your household.

- Use shared drive time to process your day with each other.

- Use some premade conversation starters at mealtime. My family unknowingly bought a package of napkins that have silly, simple conversation starters printed on them. They've led to some surprising conversations around the table.

- Start giving deeper words of encouragement to people in your household. In our learning lab at church we started what we called "Operation Tychicus." Inspired by the biblical character Tychicus's ability to "encourage hearts" (Colossians 4:7-9; Ephesians 6:21-22) and seeing the refrain in the New Testament to "encourage one another" (1 Thessalonians 4:18, 5:11; 2 Corinthians 13:11; Hebrews 3:13), we set out to start giving (sometimes deep) words of encouragement to the folks in our own households. This actually seeded spiritual conversations.

There's a variety of small things you could do to provide some light fare and whet people's appetites for more hearty conversation.

Provide a steady diet. Want to provide a steady diet of healthy food? Just make sure your fridge and cupboards are stocked with plenty of the basics: starches and proteins and veggies. You always want to have plenty of healthy essentials on hand. That's how you provide for a healthy diet.

Helping a household relate to each other in healthy, sustainable ways is not unlike that approach to having plenty of solid meat-and-potato entrées available. It's about the regular provision of healthy conversation—conversation that in the normal course of life moves beyond mere chatting into some of the joys and pains of life and even some of how Jesus is a part of everyday life. Here are some ways you could provide a steady (and regularly recurring) diet of spiritual conversations in your own household:

- Have a weekly check-in when everyone in the household can share what they have in the coming week.

- If your household goes to church together, start the practice of sharing a meal afterwards. Spend time talking about the message you heard during the service.

- Establish a mealtime rhythm in the evening: at the start of dinner everyone shares a high and low from their day. (You don't even have to tell them that a daily rhythm of reflecting on "consolation and desolation" is an ancient Ignatian practice!)

- Ask everyone on a regular basis (perhaps at bedtime or before heading off for the day) how you can pray for them—which can lead to wonderful regular conversations *and* more prayers.

- Use some premade conversation starters that are a little deeper in nature or are explicitly Christian. When I was a child there was only *The Ungame*, but these days there are lots of deeper, even Christian, conversation starters available that you could keep on the table or in the car to use during the day.

Whatever your regular diet of conversation is, it doesn't have to always take you to the deep end of the pool. There are great ways of implementing rhythms in life that get you and those in your household talking about the joys and pains of life and even how Jesus is a part of your everyday life.

Offer a rich dessert. No one can live solely on dessert— even though we sometimes wish we could. But there is something special and important about the richness and delight of dessert. There is something bonding about engaging in an extravagant dessert with others that can bond you in ways regular meat-and-potatoes never could.

Sometimes inviting your family into a deeper, more vulnerable, and honest spiritual conversation is just like this: while you can't force it, you sure can offer it. And all of that chatting you've done and all of that regular, honest sharing you've done is what paves the way for these rich, blessed encounters. Here are some ways you could offer rich conversation into your household's life from time to time:

- Go out to a one-on-one meal with someone in your household. While we all love eating together as a family, certain conversations will only happen when there are just two of you at the table.

- Invite some innately deep, spiritual, mature Christian friends to a meal with your household—their natural depth creates space for others to follow suit.

- Explicitly invite your household into a deeper conversation on special occasions. I distinctly remember when one Christmas Eve when my father had our normally quiet household get hot chocolate and sit in the den, and each of us shared one thing we were proud of each other for from the last year. This was scary, unchartered territory for us, but we did it!

- Write a long, thoughtful letter to someone in your household and see how they respond. Sometimes communicating in a written format gives people more time and space to get honest. There is something about asynchronous communication (no immediate back-and-forth) that can provide the space for people to get deeper than they normally would.

- Do a craft together where you each have to create a picture or poem or small sculpture that represents, for example, how your faith is doing. There's something about art that allows us to discern and communicate deep things that normally can't quite be captured in words.

- Go camping or hiking—an extended group activity that is screen-free and provides plenty of unhurried time for conversation.

In these and other ways you could offer rich dessert to your family, creating opportunities for people to indulge in deep, spiritual conversations.

CAN I REALLY HAVE A LOUD TABLE IN MY HOUSEHOLD?

As I experienced while driving to dinner with my dad all those years ago, you can't force someone to have a conversation. But you can set the table and invite them to it. And you can start with light fare and whet the appetite. Offer a bit of light food, and you never know just what might happen.

Thankfully, my dad didn't give up on me after I chose silence while driving to dinner that one summer night. He kept inviting me to chat, to share, and even to get deep on occasion. My dad's a boomer (and a dad!) and I'm an introvert, so we've got some of the spiritual conversation cards stacked against us. But I'm glad to say we've been growing over the years.

If having spiritual conversations as a household seems like a daunting new endeavor, remember that this household habit is really quite old, and it is how God intended households to function from the very beginning. Your household is made for this.

Not only is your household made for a loud table, remember that Jesus came to help us relate to each other. As we take practical steps to nurture loud tables in our homes, it can be encouraging to remember that Jesus worked (and works) to help us with this task.

Jesus came to earth to help us reconcile with each other and be in a healthy relationship with each other. As he put it, "This is my commandment, that you love one another as I have loved you" (John 15:12). Through Jesus' sacrifice on the cross, he reconciled us to God, but this had the additional effect of reconciling us to each other.

Jesus also sent us the gift of the Holy Spirit so that we could grow and heal our relationships. Think of, for example, the fruits of the Holy Spirit. What is the Spirit naturally laboring for and producing within the lives of redeemed Christians? Paul's list is predominantly relational in its implications: "The fruit of the Spirit is love, joy, peace, patience, kindness, goodness, faithfulness, gentleness, self-control; against such things there is no law" (Galatians 5:22-23).

Jesus also modeled healthy, intimate relationships. He lived with and among people, touched lepers, shared table fellowship with outcasts, felt deeply the pains of the people around him: sighing, being moved by compassion, weeping. Jesus didn't merely broadcast his teachings to crowds; he went a step further and invited people to come closer to him, to be with him in a more intimate way. Jesus didn't only exchange theories with other teachers; he talked with men and women—and children!—about his kingdom. And he quite often did this by having spiritual conversations in the everyday homes of those he was talking with.

Jesus' model of relating to the people around him should not be taken lightly. His habit of eating meals with people was one of the early habits that got him in trouble with the religious rulers of the day. His manner among men and women stood out as revolutionary. His teachings about forgiveness and patience became the centerpiece of most early Christian writings and were perhaps one of the reasons so many people were drawn to him and the church grew rapidly in spite of such hostile circumstances in its first centuries.[20]

Not only is your household made to have spiritual conversations, but Jesus came to help us do just that. When we seek to grow and nurture our household's relationships with each other, we are simply joining Jesus in what he is working toward with us every day.

In other words, the table is set and the food is ready. Spiritual conversations are something every single person in our household is already hungry for because they were made for such intimacy. God wants us to relate to each other in intimacy. And the more we do, the more spiritually vibrant our homes will become.

HOW CAN I PURSUE FOCUSED GROWTH IN THIS AREA?

Obviously, family and interpersonal dynamics affect how you might go about pursuing greater intimacy in a household. There might be seasons when such growth seems impossible or at least an outside professional's help is needed. Given that, if you are in a season when helping your household relate to each other is something you want to spend some significant time growing in, the following are a few resources inspired by this latest research to help you pursue personal growth in this area.

- Don Everts, "How to Talk About Your Faith: An Introduction to the Spiritual Conversation Curve," (Lutheran Hour Ministries, 2019). This practical, biblically based conversation model can not only help you approach spiritual conversations of an evangelistic nature but can give you handles on how to nurture deeper spiritual conversations with anyone over time. This booklet can be found at www.lhm.org/households.

- Don Everts, *The Reluctant Witness: Discovering the Delight of Spiritual Conversations* (Downers Grove, IL: InterVarsity Press, 2019). With original research from the Barna Group on spiritual conversations in the digital age, this book offers fresh insights and best practices for how to become an eager conversationalist.

- "Helping Your Child Have Spiritual Conversations." Parents have high hopes for their children's faith, but they don't always know how to get them there. This booklet helps parents grow their child's faith through spiritual conversations by discovering how to use Jesus' methods and cover Jesus' topics in conversations in their everyday lives. This booklet can be found at www .lhm.org/households.

- "Daily Devotions." These devotions from Lutheran Hour Ministries will help strengthen and encourage your faith as you do the same for others. Perfect for personal reflection or to share with your whole household. Each devotion ends with discussion questions designed to spark a spiritual conversation. For more information go to www.lhm.org/dailydevotions.

- "Vibrant Conversations Deck." In light of the findings related to spiritual conversations, Lutheran Hour Ministries developed this working deck of cards. Not only can these cards be used to play your favorite card games, but they contain fifty-two great questions in four categories: applying spiritual disciplines, extending hospitality, engaging in spiritual conversations, and food and fun. You can use these cards to spark spiritual conversations around your own table, in the car, or wherever your household is gathered together. This deck can be found at www.lhm.org/households.

OPEN DOORS

HELPING OUR HOUSEHOLDS EXTEND HOSPITALITY

The LORD your God is God of gods and Lord of lords, the great, the mighty, and the awesome God, who is not partial and takes no bribe. He executes justice for the fatherless and the widow, and loves the sojourner, giving him food and clothing. Love the sojourner, therefore, for you were sojourners in the land of Egypt.

DEUTERONOMY 10:17-19

Wendy and I were three years into the suburban dream when we started to feel antsy. When we were called to serve at a suburban church we had done what we had been trained to do: incarnate. We moved into the neighborhood. Since all the neighborhoods around the church were suburban, this meant that Wendy and the kids and I became a suburban family.

Parts of this were wonderful: a quiet street for our kids to play on and great schools for them to go to. Plenty of nearby shopping, including options for buying healthy food. Low crime rates—at least low rates of certain kinds of crimes. (We later found out that drug use was rampant in suburbia.) Suburbia had its own temptations and liabilities, of course: the syrup of suburbia started to coat us and our kids with entitlement at an alarming rate. But all in all, it was a beautiful place to live.

And then we got antsy. This wasn't wanderlust or boredom. Rather, Wendy and I both started to feel that inexorable, numinous, complex, undeniable thing some refer to as a "call." We both independently felt called to invite my mother and stepfather (Nancy and Buzz, who lived far away in Washington state) to move in with our family. Buzz was teetering on the edge of being medically fragile, and it was becoming too much for my mom to handle on her own. Neither Nancy nor Buzz had ever been people of much means, being hard workers who hadn't gotten many breaks. A devastating car crash early in life had left Buzz partially paralyzed and dealing with a wide variety of ailments. My mom was doing what she could to care for him, but her physical and financial resources weren't limitless.

The calling felt clear to Wendy and me: we should open our door and invite them into our household. That's how, three years into our suburban journey, we went from a household of five (plus one cat) to a household of seven (plus two cats). It turned out to be the most rewarding and costly thing we had ever done.

Since getting married, Wendy and I had always had a fairly hospitable household. Our main impediments to hospitality had been our modest missionary income and my introversion. The modest income was easily overcome: Wendy is not only a great and creative cook (able to make a feast from a humble cupboard) but is the only person I know who will barter at stores that don't do bartering. Our first significant table as a couple was a spectacularly long, three-leaf table with eight matching chairs that Wendy bartered for at our local thrift store. (We still have that glorious table!)

My introversion has been a much tougher obstacle. Having relational jobs has tended to leave me relationally tapped once I get home. But a combination of God's work in my life (including inviting me to obey the Sabbath command) and Wendy's patient partnership has allowed us to open our door with some fashion of regularity. Not only have we regularly welcomed people into our home for feasts and festivities, but we have also had numerous housemates live with us and nurtured significant relationships with neighbors over the years.

But even for us, having Nancy and Buzz move in was a stretch—for us and for them. Overnight they went from a quiet household of two semi-retired adults to an active, bustling (loud) household of young kids. I became something of a carpenter: with the help of many, many friends I slowly turned our two-car garage into "The West Wing," as we call it—a four-room suite for Nancy and Buzz. Wendy became something of a social worker: patiently helping Nancy and Buzz get the care, counsel, services, and encouragement they needed. And our kids were asked to sacrifice. They not only lost their garage (it was serving as a play, craft, mess-around place for them) but also their basement (the finished basement became an apartment for Nancy and Buzz for the two years while the West Wing was under construction).

During this transition, plenty of people asked us, with genuine concern, "What are you guys doing?" During the toughest times, Wendy and I asked the same question. Our suburban context, after all, encourages isolation. Isolation has long been understood as endemic to the suburban ethos.[1] Suburbanites have social buffers built around their lives (think large yards, porches on the back of the house instead of the front, attached garages, plenty of money to not have to ask for much help), and this isolation has, from the beginning of the suburban experiment, been seen as a virtue. This isn't only happening in suburbia, of course. As Lesslie Newbigin observes about life in the West, "Western European civilisation has witnessed a sort of atomising process, in which the individual is more and more set free from his natural setting in family and neighborhood, and becomes a sort of replaceable unit in the social machine. His nearest neighbors may not even know his name."[2]

And as if these cultural biases toward isolation weren't enough, in our post-Christian world there is an increasing temptation as Christians to close ourselves off from others.

Rather than have our households relate to the wider world around us, many are being tempted to "circle the wagons" and close our Christian households off from neighbors and institutions and influences that seem less and less friendly to the Christian faith.

Entire books have been written calling Christians to a "strategic withdrawal" from mainstream society to avoid the influence of a seemingly less and less Christian America.[3] These books are selling well. As Brenda Colijn points out, "In response to cultural pressures, some parts of the American church have promoted the nuclear family as a haven or fortress that keeps out the values and stresses of the world."[4] In a time when many are suffering from "chronic loneliness," Christians are being tempted to close their doors because of the cultural influences outside those doors.

Add all this up and you can understand why there were a variety of voices (including ours from time to time) asking, "What are you guys doing?" But even when the voices were strongest, even when the house felt too full, we were confident that relating to the wider world with purpose was a normal thing for a household to do. In fact, we had a strong sense that opening our door wide with hospitality was how God had designed us to live.

And, indeed, throughout the Bible God makes it clear that his people are intended to relate to the world around them with wide hospitality.

ARE WE MEANT TO RELATE TO THE
WIDER WORLD AS A HOUSEHOLD?

Let's return one final time to the Plains of Moab. During their seminal time with God before entering the Promised Land, God's people were called into a living relationship with him (see chap. four) and were invited to regularly talk about and nurture that within their homes (see chap. five). It is noteworthy that as God is giving his people a vision for what it means to be his people, he also called them to a life of hospitality based on God's own hospitable ways. God spelled it out plainly at Moab, telling his people that he "loves the sojourner," and so they too should "love the sojourner" (Deuteronomy 10:18-19).

This echoes what God had made clear forty years earlier on Mt. Sinai, "When a stranger sojourns with you in your land, you shall not do him wrong. You shall treat the stranger who sojourns with you as the native among you, and you shall love him as yourself, for you were strangers in the land of Egypt: I am the LORD your God" (Leviticus 19:33-34).

The Israelites were to take new people (like travelers and widows and orphans) into their extended households because they are in a living relationship with a hospitable God. The value of hospitality was unambiguous and practical and robust. God wasn't calling his people to give to the needy from a distance but to open wide their doors and welcome them into their own homes with love.

It was clear that hospitality was an essential part of God's people's spiritual life. In Isaiah we read that an "acceptable fast"

is . . . to share your bread with the hungry
and bring the homeless poor into your house.
(Isaiah 58:7)

In the same chapter God was clear that his people would themselves be blessed by giving themselves over to a life of hospitality:

If you pour yourself out for the hungry
and satisfy the desire of the afflicted,
then shall your light rise in the darkness
and your gloom be as noonday. (Isaiah 58:10)

So clear was the call to open wide their doors with hospitality that Job included hospitality in defense of his way of life, pointing out that

the sojourner has not lodged in the street;
I have opened my doors to the traveler. (Job 31:32)

In calling his people to a life of hospitality, God was inviting his people to a purpose close to his own heart and central to his own mission in the world. As Varghese points out, "God's character should be reflected in the life of Israel, including caring for and doing justice for the alien."[5]

And this call to a wide, purposeful hospitality didn't change when Jesus came. If anything, it intensified.

Jesus, after all, was critiqued for how welcoming he was to marginalized characters: he ate with sinners, touched lepers, stopped to notice and care for widows. And he encouraged others to do the same. On one occasion he was quite explicit that we shouldn't just open our door to wealthy neighbors who will invite us back to their place, "But when you give a feast, invite the poor, the crippled, the lame, the blind, and you will be blessed, because they cannot repay you. For you will be repaid at the resurrection of the just" (Luke 14:13-14).

Here Jesus strikes the same two notes that were struck in Isaiah (and throughout the Old Testament): we are called to open our doors to others, and when we do, *we* will be blessed.

No wonder this became a hallmark of the Christian church. The early church was known for the love, generosity, and welcome they showed to those in need. They had open doors. This habit of hospitality didn't just happen, it was a central part of their understanding of the Christian life. For example, look how the author of Hebrews expressed the call to Christian hospitality: "Do not neglect to show hospitality to strangers, for thereby some have entertained angels unawares" (Hebrews 13:2).

It is interesting to note that the Greek word here in Hebrews 13 that we translate as "hospitality" is *philoxenia*. It comes from two Greek roots: *philos* (loving) and *xenos* (a stranger).[6] Hospitality is the act of loving the stranger, being predisposed to having affection for the outsider. This is exactly what God called his people to do at Moab: love the sojourner. And so his people did.

Hospitality was an explicit habit in the early church. The call to Christian hospitality was unambiguous: "Contribute to the needs of the saints and seek to show hospitality" (Romans 12:13). "Above all, keep loving one another earnestly, since love covers a multitude of sins. Show hospitality to one another without grumbling" (1 Peter 4:8-9).

The early church understood that they were called to live out the Christian mission right at their dinner table. As Jen Pollock Michel puts it, "Our redemption story is bound up with the housekeeping of a table. In our homes we keep the feast by offering God's welcome to others: not only family and friends, Jesus said, but the needy stranger."[7]

It bears note, too, that hospitality is a two-way street. When we open our doors, we may be lending a hand to those in need, but we are also enriched in the process. We need others as much as they need us. Paul was unambiguous in his language: "There are many parts, yet one body. The eye cannot say to the hand, 'I have no need of you,' nor again the head to the feet, 'I have no need of you'" (1 Corinthians 12:20-21). Paul goes on to clarify that the parts of the body that seem weaker are actually indispensable to the body.

Part of what is so blessed about Christian hospitality (over against other good acts of mercy like almsgiving) is that it brings people into connection with each other. As Butterfield points out, "This gospel call that renders strangers into neighbors into family of God . . . requires both hosts and guests.

We must participate as both hosts and guests—not just one or the other—as giving and receiving are good and sacred and connect people and communities in important ways."[8]

Hospitality blesses those being welcomed and those doing the welcoming. Even in the costlier moments of having Nancy and Buzz live with us, Wendy and I couldn't deny the joy and abundant life each of us experienced in this act of hospitality. Serving Nancy and Buzz brought us joy. And having them in our extended family blessed us with the unique gifts and perspectives (and a penchant for corny jokes, in the case of Buzz) that have enriched our lives and the lives of our kids and others in our extended household.

Not only is it clear throughout the Bible that we are to open wide our doors with hospitality, but it is also clear that by doing this, God's people will bless the wider world and will be blessed in return.

WHICH IS BETTER: A SAFE SUBMARINE OR A RISKY RESCUE SHIP?

There is something simultaneously exciting and scary about this call to hospitality. The impulse to circle the wagons may neglect our call to hospitality, but it is comforting. Our world is a scary place, and for Christians in an increasingly post-Christian West it seems to get scarier all the time.

The fact is most Christians are less familiar with God's call to *philoxenia* and more familiar with the common cultural call to *xenophobia*, another Greek word also made up of two Greek roots: *xenos* (a stranger) and *phobos* (fear). Rather than being predisposed to loving the stranger as our God calls us to, we can often be predisposed to fear the stranger.

There is something understandable about fearing strangers, of course. What parent hasn't tried to instill a helpful fear of strangers in their child's young heart? We do this to protect our children because there are some bad people out there. It is interesting to note, though, that rather than instilling *discernment* in our children (how do you tell who to trust?) we naturally instill *fear* (all strangers are bad).

The reality is loving strangers is actually costly. Many of our family moments became awkward or interrupted because of Buzz's varying health needs. Our kids lost their garage and the basement. Isolation has its perks. Having a shut door keeps the noise and the need of the outside world at bay. It may grow stuffy inside, but what's a little stale air when compared with the messiness of the outside world clomping its muddy boots into our living room?

You can see the appeal, I'm sure. Keeping the door shut is safe and comforting and makes life more neat and predictable. The difference between this comforting model and the biblical model, it seems to me, is similar to the difference between a rescue ship and a submarine.

With a submarine we are nicely contained and dry. We are protected from the various dangers of the sea and the world.

We may be in the ocean, but we don't have to get wet. Or cold. Or windblown. Or interrupted by nearby ships. A submarine's primary virtue is that it is completely sealed and can therefore sink down from the waves and weather and other ships into the calm below the surface. There are fewer external variables to deal with. Outside of water pressure, a submarine is in a fairly controlled environment.

For Christians this can be compelling. Especially when we consider that in his high priestly prayer Jesus makes it clear that his followers are "not of this world" and are therefore "hated" by the world around them (John 17:14). Add in the fact that Jesus goes on to pray that his followers would be "sanctified" in the truth (sanctified means "to be made holy" or "to be made separate"), and we can understand why some choose to live a submarine sort of Christian life marked by *xenophobia*—fear of the stranger.

The biblical call to *philoxenia*—love of the stranger—is much more wide open and messy and unpredictable. Kind of like sailing the seas in a rescue ship: exposed to the air and wind and weather, seeking flailing vessels or castaways floating on timbers, barely keeping their heads above water. Not only are we open to the elements, but we are purposefully pulling alongside struggling people and throwing a lifeline to them. We lower the rope ladder and welcome them onto the ship.

And who knows what kind of appetite or weird habits or strange diseases they may carry with them? Life on a rescue ship is inherently unpredictable and messy. Our door is purposefully left wide open to the storm-tossed, needy world. And in this fallen world that is a scary prospect.

But even though sailing on a rescue ship is not neat or predictable, I have to admit there's something so captivating and *alive* about a life oriented around others. There is something electric and exhilarating about a kingdom rescue ship, opening wide the door of hospitality. Rosaria Butterfield beautifully describes this biblical call to adventurous hospitality:

> Instead of feeling sidelined by the sucker punches of post-Christianity, Christians are called to practice radically ordinary hospitality to renew their resolve in Christ. Too many of us are sidelined by fears. We fear that people will hurt us. We fear that people will negatively influence our children. . . . We long for days gone by. Our sentimentality makes us stupid. We need to snap ourselves out of this self-pitying reverie. The best days are ahead. Jesus advances from the front of the line.[9]

While the submarine and strategic retreat from the world are appealing, the Bible is clear that we are meant to sail through this world on a mission, not afraid of what may come. After all, in that same high priestly prayer, Jesus was unambiguous when he prayed to the Father, "I do not ask that you take them out of the world. . . . As you sent me into the world, so I have sent them into the world" (John 17:15, 18).

Let's remember that God did not send Jesus into the world in a hermetically sealed submarine. He sent him into the seas of human need to rescue those who were drowning. And so we, too, are sent by Jesus. It's to be the rescue ship, not the submarine. And the research supports this.

WHAT DO WE LEARN ABOUT RELATING WITH THE WIDER WORLD FROM SPIRITUALLY VIBRANT HOMES?

Remember there are three distinct household habits that correspond with greater spiritual vibrancy. The first two we've already looked at closely: applying spiritual disciplines and engaging in spiritual conversations. The last of our three habits that emerged from the research was perhaps the most surprising. It's a household habit the researchers called, simply, "hospitality"—what we're calling the open door (fig. 6.1).

Spiritually vibrant homes practice hospitality. This hospitality is multifaceted: it not only involves blessing others by welcoming them into the extended household but also involves *being blessed* by these newcomers to the household. So, people in spiritually vibrant homes have open doors, but what exactly does that look like?

When we pull back the curtains and look inside vibrant households practicing hospitality, what do we learn?

Finding 1. Hospitality is connected to God's mission.
There is something about recognizing the importance of God's

rescue mission that is related to the habit of hospitality in Christian homes. The researchers found that "a sense of responsibility to tell others about one's Christian beliefs is common among those who have regular guests."[10] It is possible that a sense of the greater kingdom rescue mission animates these households, making them more invitational and

FIGURE 6.1

hospitable. For Wendy and me, God's mission of love has been a huge factor in our own everyday practice of hospitality.

Christian hospitality can benefit the Christian mission. Varghese describes some of this connection, "The household of God reflects the character of God by extending hospitality to those who are not part of their family. This will bring people, poor, lame, crippled and blind, who are rejected and ignored by society into the kingdom where they will experience the love of God."[11] The connection between Christian hospitality and the Christian mission led John Piper to come up with the term *strategic hospitality*. He observes,

> What I mean by strategic hospitality is a hospitality that thinks strategically and asks: How can I draw the most people into a deep experience of God's hospitality by the use of my home or my church home? Who might need reinforcements just now in the battle against loneliness? Who are the people who could be brought together in my home most strategically for the sake of the kingdom? . . .
>
> Strategic hospitality is not content to just have the old clan over for dinner again and again.[12]

Spiritually vibrant homes are, it turns out, not content to have the old clan over again and again. Their doors are open explicitly because of God's mission, which they see themselves as having a part in.

1. When have you experienced or seen an example of not just recreational hospitality but "strategic hospitality" as Piper describes it?

2. On a scale of one to ten (where one is a calm bystander and ten is an active partner), describe your household's engagement with God's mission.

3. As you ask the specific questions Piper poses, are there any faces or names in your life that come to mind?

Finding 2. Hospitality strengthens faith formation. If you find the connection between everyday hospitality and the Christian mission to be somewhat surprising, you might find this *really* surprising: there is also a connection between extending hospitality and having a vibrant faith. Here the researchers actually suggest causality: "Generally, faith formation is connected to and increases with a spirit of hospitality."[13] Welcoming households are prone to foster spiritual development more than nonwelcoming households.

The irony is that in trying to protect our Christian faith from the outside world, we may be inadvertently weakening that very faith. Parents who are sheltering their children in a submarine for the sake of their spiritual growth may actually be slowing their spiritual growth. Isolation is actually a risk factor for spiritual vibrancy.

The stale air of a Christian submarine does not seem to correlate with the kind of spiritual growth that comes with the brisk ocean air of hospitality—even if that hospitality is costly in other ways. Perhaps this shouldn't surprise us. As the Bible's wisdom told us long ago, "Whoever isolates himself seeks his own desire; he breaks out against all sound judgment" (Proverbs 18:1).

> **1.** On a scale of one to ten (where one is very isolated and ten is very hospitable), how would you describe your household? In what ways are "fear of the stranger" or "love of the stranger" nurtured within your household?
>
> **2.** How many times a year do you invite someone new into your home or just drop in at someone else's house?
>
> **3.** Are there features of your current season in life that make extending hospitality understandably more difficult right now?

Finding 3. Hospitality enlarges the extended household in helpful ways. Hospitality brings more people into a household's orbit, which can greatly improve faith formation within that household. The researchers found that households with outside voices are more likely to have a vibrant faith than those who do not have outside guests. These guests are often, but not always, relatives, as figure 6.2 illustrates.

Whether or not you are inviting people in to care for their needs, it turns out their presence in your household strengthens the faith of those in your household. Perhaps Frederick

TOP FIVE FREQUENT VISITORS FOR EACH TYPE OF HOUSEHOLD

	Nuclear family household	Single-parent household	Multi-generational household	Roommate household	Couple household	Other household
1	A close friend 26%	A close friend 25%	A close friend 25%	A close friend 26%	Adult child 29%	A close friend 20%
2	Sibling 15%	Sibling 19%	Sibling 17%	Sibling 15%	Grandchild 23%	Sibling 13%
3	Mother 14%	Mother 14%	Neighbor 17%	Neighbor 11%	A close friend 15%	Mother 12%
4	Grandparent 13%	Neighbor 12%	Other relative 11%	Boyfriend or girlfriend 9%	Son- / daughter-in-law 14%	Other relative 12%
5	Neighbor 10%	Child's close friend 11%	Grandchild 10%	Mother 8%	Neighbor 10%	Neighbor 10%

n=2,347 US practicing Christian adults and teens, April 5–11, 2018.

FIGURE 6.2

Buechner was right when he observed that "When Jesus commanded us to love our neighbors as ourselves, it was not just for our neighbors' sakes that he commanded it, but for our own sakes as well."[14] There are a variety of ways these outside voices are helpful, as the researchers concluded:

> One way or another, Christians need outside influences for robust faith formation. Adults whose upbringing did not plant them in meaningful Christian teachings or traditions might grow in community with their extended households. Meanwhile, adults with a long-held Christian identity might look to resources and voices beyond their family of origin to re-examine or strengthen their beliefs.[15]

I can personally testify to how Nancy and Buzz's devoted prayer life has been a model for my own children.

1. Who are the most frequent visitors in your home?

2. How have you and your household been blessed by guests or members of your extended household?

3. Do you have any household members who started out as guests? How did they become a more central part of your household over time?

Finding 4. Spiritually vibrant homes rely on others.

Another interesting correlation from the research is that

people in spiritually vibrant homes are more likely to depend on others for help. Dependence may not intuitively seem to relate to spiritual vibrancy, but vibrant households are more likely to depend on others for practical help (like finances, childcare, and other needs) and are also quicker to name either family or nonfamily members as people they go to for advice or encouragement.

In figure 6.3 you can compare the level of dependence between "vibrant households" (where all three household habits are present), "hospitable households" (where only hospitality, the third habit, is present), and "dormant households" (where none of the habits are present). As you can see, hospitable households and spiritually vibrant households are more likely to depend on others. Again, no causality but an interesting correlation.

In the New Testament, Paul uses body language to describe the intended interdependence the church is to have: lots of different members bring different gifts to the table. Paul also underscores how each member needs the others. This dynamic would seem to be very much in play in households that practice hospitality. I can personally attest to how our own ventures into hospitality have actually required us to lean more on others. We are less self-sufficient because of our open door. Hospitality has actually caused us to interact with, depend on, and be blessed by people we may never have run into otherwise— exactly what Paul's body metaphor describes.[16]

VIBRANT HOUSEHOLDS ARE MORE LIKELY TO LEAN ON OTHERS

DO YOU DEPEND ON FAMILY MEMBERS WHO DO NOT LIVE IN YOUR HOME TO HELP WITH FINANCES, CHILDCARE, OR OTHER THINGS TO KEEP YOUR HOUSEHOLD RUNNING?

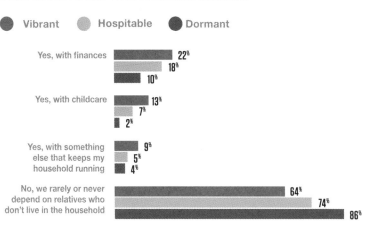

● Vibrant   ● Hospitable   ● Dormant

Yes, with finances
- 22%
- 18%
- 10%

Yes, with childcare
- 13%
- 7%
- 2%

Yes, with something else that keeps my household running
- 9%
- 5%
- 4%

No, we rarely or never depend on relatives who don't live in the household
- 64%
- 74%
- 86%

n=1,899 US practicing Christian adults, April 5–11, 2018.

PERCENT INDICATES HAVING ANY HOUSEHOLD RELATIONSHIP THAT THEY ARE LIKELY TO GO TO FOR...

Advice
- 96%
- 91%
- 76%

Sympathy
- 91%
- 80%
- 69%

Encouragement
- 90%
- 89%
- 74%

Logistical help
- 88%
- 81%
- 66%

n=2,347 US practicing Christian adult and teens, April 5–11, 2018.

FIGURE 6.3

> **1.** How do you depend on family members or others who do not live in your home to help with finances, childcare, or other things to keep your household running?
>
> **2.** Who are those in your household likely to go to for advice, sympathy, encouragement, or logistical help?
>
> **3.** In your household (and in your heart) is dependency viewed as more of a liability or a virtue? Why do you think that is?

Finding 5. Some people struggle with hospitality. We don't have to use much imagination to discern that some people, by temperament or biography alone, may find a life on the high seas of hospitality more difficult: introverts, people who have been burned by others, those who tend to be more fearful, those living in a particularly hostile or unsafe environment.

Sometimes our life situation may make hospitality more difficult to imagine or extend. While insularity can exist anywhere (40 percent of those surveyed say that nobody comes to spend time with them frequently), there is a higher incidence of isolation among couple households (see fig. 6.4). Often the larger or busier a household is (think children in the home), the less insular the household.

Insularity is not uncommon, of course. A full 31 percent of all Americans admit they have no one in their local area,

"NO ONE COMES TO MY HOME ON A REGULAR BASIS"

- ● Couple household
- ● Roommate household
- ● Nuclear family household
- ● Single-parent household
- ○ Multigenerational household
- ○ Other

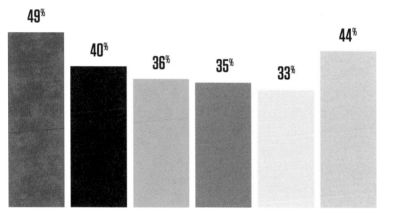

49% 40% 36% 35% 33% 44%

FIGURE 6.4

outside of family members, who they could rely on for help in the case of an emergency or tough situation.[17] But some situations in life tend to cultivate a more insular lifestyle: couple households (primarily made up of older boomers and elders) are fairly isolated, for example, whereas younger millennials tend to value opening their homes and do just that.[18] Whether by temperament, season of life, or household type, it is important to be aware of barriers to hospitality.

> **1.** Do you agree or disagree with the statement "No one comes to my home on a regular basis"?
>
> **2.** If you are a part of someone else's extended household, how regularly do you go into their home?
>
> **3.** What barriers to hospitality do you or others in your household currently have?

HOW CAN I HELP MY HOUSEHOLD EXTEND HOSPITALITY?

When turning our thoughts from what the Bible and research have to say about hospitality to what that can look like in our own households, we should be wary of stressful list checking. It must be possible to ask the question, How can I help my household extend hospitality? without falling into some duty-bound dirge.

Perhaps the image of an open door can be helpful here. The submarine and rescue ship really are two poles of what is in reality a spectrum on how closed or open a door can be. Is the door of your household tightly shut with the lock bolted? That's the submarine. Have you blown the doors off your household? That's the rescue ship on the high seas.

But the reality is, most of us are somewhere between those two extremes. We aren't hermits, but we also aren't always hospitable or as hospitable as we want to be. The problem is, the folks inside a home are typically quite acclimated to the temperature and atmosphere of the home. In other words, we don't always welcome having our door opened wider than it currently is.

I think of all the times my kids have been playing outside (having a great time) and burst through the front door happily inviting me to get off the couch and come join them. Whether it's summer or winter my first instinct is to cry out, "Shut the door!" They may be used to the temperature outside, but I'm not!

In a similar way, it can be a little too much to blow the doors off your household's hospitality all at once. If your household is more accustomed to a closed door, start by cracking the door just a little. It's amazing what a little fresh air can do to make you realize just how stale it's gotten inside. Once the door is cracked, you can then proceed to open the door wider, a little at a time. The idea is to step into what God has for your household and its purposeful relationship with the wider world. By opening a little wider, you can do just that. And, sure, maybe for some households that have more of an open door, there are times when God may call them to blow the door right off its hinges and alter forever the hospitality habits of their home.

Whether cracking the door, opening the door a little wider, or blowing the doors off, we can do all these things, with God's help, in our very own homes (fig. 6.5).

The Spiritually
Vibrant Home

MESSY PRAYERS

LOUD TABLES

OPEN DOORS

1. Crack the door
2. Open a little wider
3. Blow the doors off

FIGURE 6.5

Crack the door. Want to introduce your household to the wider world around it? Just crack the door. If your household tends to be fairly insular, it is possible to ease your way into moments of hospitality. Here are some ways you could crack open the door of hospitality just a little bit in your own home:

- Host a dinner party for friends.

- Offer to host the next extended family gathering at your house.

- Drop in at a friend or relative's home unannounced. If you need an excuse, bake some fresh cookies and bring them over as an unexpected treat.

- On a household calendar keep track of every person who comes into your house each month. Just being more mindful of the people God is bringing within the orbit of your household can help.

- Have everyone in your household make a "relationship map" of their lives: drawing a circle in the center of the paper for themselves and then drawing a line out from them to the various friends, acquaintances, and neighbors they have around them. Even this small task can get them thinking about the wider world around them.

- Pray regularly for some of the people on your relationship maps. You could even mark on the map when you've prayed for someone and continue this until you've prayed for everyone on your maps.

- The next time you need an ingredient for a recipe, try walking next door to borrow rather than simply heading to the store to purchase.

There's a variety of small things you could do to crack the door of hospitality a little bit and see how little moments of hospitality can bring in some fresh air (and a reminder of the wider world) into your lives.

Open a little wider. If you are accustomed to having moments of hospitality, you can push the door a little wider to develop some regular habits of hospitality. Here are some ways you could open your door a little wider:

- Start throwing a specific kind of party and make a tradition of it (a New Year's Eve party, Super Bowl party, themed birthday parties—even for the adults in your household).

- Buy a guest book that everyone who comes into your home can sign. Pray about a goal for how many guests you want to sign it in the next twelve months.

- Take regular dinner parties a step further by always inviting one or two new people every time you have friends over. You could look on your relationship map and choose someone you've never had over before.

- Pick a day of the week when you will always stop by someone else's house to simply check in to see how they are doing. Again, bringing fresh cookies never hurts.

- Organize a game night or movie night and invite widely— try to get every seat in your home filled.

- The next time you have a household need, think creatively about a person you already know who you could invite over to help you meet the need rather than simply paying a professional to take care of it. Even if you could afford to simply pay a professional, why not invite someone from the neighborhood or church or work who has a specialty in a certain area?

- Next time you hear of someone with a household need, go to their place and offer to roll up your sleeves and help them with it.

- Choose a young family that might be overwhelmed with the frenzy of raising kids and look for ways to bless them as a guest in their household.

There are a wide variety of things you could do to develop some habits of hospitality that push your door open a little wider all the time.

Blow the doors off. It may be too much to go from submarine to rescue ship in one day, but some of our households that are already moderately hospitable can do something more trajectory changing to go from having some hospitable habits to being hospitality shaped as a household. Here are some ways you could blow the doors off your own home:

- Buy a bigger table and more chairs. This may seem simple, but that huge table Wendy got for us at a thrift store early in our married life actually made hosting lots of people a more common occurrence for us.

- Rearrange your home to be more hospitable. You don't have to have a huge home to do this. As a college student I saw students loft dorm beds and move desks into closets so that they could regularly host more people.

- Move to a home that is more hospitable. Wesley Hill tells the story a single woman in her early forties who purposefully bought a house with a large dining room and filled it with a large table so that she could be hospitable. As Hill wrote, "I now have at least one strong, happy memory of it seeming like the most normal thing in the world for a single person to buy a house with a big dining room, make sure that the room is furnished with an extendable table and plenty of extra chairs, and invite people from outside her own life situation to be her guests."[19]

- Invite your mom and stepdad to move in with you!

- Become a state-approved foster family.

- Host an exchange student.

- Informally adopt a young family from your church or neighborhood. Wendy and I have been so blessed by a few adoptive grandparents and adoptive aunts and uncles who have cared for us and our kids in amazing ways—there are seasons we could not have gotten through without them.

- Informally adopt an elderly person from your church or neighborhood. When Wendy found out that an elderly neighbor in the next condo over in Boulder was struggling to feed herself, she started making our meals a little larger, bought some Tupperware, and brought food over every night for two years.

You could make decisions like these that would forever alter the shape of your household's hospitality.

CAN I REALLY HAVE AN OPEN DOOR IN MY HOUSEHOLD?

It is a joy to report, eight years into our new adventure with the West Wing, that Wendy and I stand amazed at how God has used our home to bless Nancy and Buzz (before he passed away) and how our home has been blessed through their presence. In this way God has been helping Wendy and me practice "radically ordinary hospitality," as Rosaria Butterfield calls it. I like Butterfield's description: "Radically ordinary hospitality is this: using your Christian home in a daily way that seeks to make strangers neighbors, and neighbors family of God. It brings glory to God, serves others, and lives out the gospel in word and deed."[20]

If extending hospitality as a household seems like a daunting new endeavor, remember that this household habit is really quite old and it is how God intended households to function from the very beginning. Your household is made for this.

Not only is your household made for an open door, remember that Jesus came to help us open our doors in blessing to the world around us. As we take practical steps to open our doors, it can be encouraging to remember that Jesus worked (and works) to help us with this task.

Jesus came to earth not only to save it but to enlist his people in that rescue mission. As he told his disciples, "You are the salt of the earth. . . . You are the light of the world" (Matthew 5:13-14). Jesus invites his people to join him in his grand rescue mission. And make no mistake, that mission is indeed grand. As Jesus put it, "You will be my witnesses in Jerusalem and in all Judea and Samaria, and to the ends of the earth" (Acts 1:8). "Whoever believes in me will do the works I have been doing, and they will do even greater things than these" (John 14:12 NIV).

And where did all of these great works transpire from the very beginning? Many of them, as we've already seen, took place in the central tool of the early church: the homes of Christians. The home was the preferred domestic laboratory for working out the mission of the church through hospitality and generosity. Jesus saw in the home not a safe haven for a nuclear family but a mission tool for extended households. As Hill put it,

> When Jesus is asked about his understanding of kinship
> and familial ties, he doesn't reject them as so much detritus

from the old regime that his kingdom is displacing. Instead, he takes the basic notion of "family" and cracks it open, stretches its contents beyond their agreed-upon limits, and wraps the result around a much wider range of people than was socially acceptable.[21]

Jesus not only calls his people into mission through hospitality, but he also equips them for that mission. Jesus sent the Holy Spirit to empower his people for their calling, giving spiritual gifts to "empower" believers (1 Corinthians 12:7-11). While my own hesitance and stubbornness to open my door to bless others is well documented, I have experienced firsthand how God equips his people for a life of hospitality.[22]

Not only is your household made to extend hospitality, but Jesus came to help you do just that. When we seek to grow and nurture our household's relationship with the wider world around us, we are simply joining Jesus in what he is working toward with us every day. And there is something sublimely beautiful about how God can help us shake off our submarine ways and join him on the high seas of his mission. John Piper observes,

> When we practice hospitality, we experience the thrill of feeling God's power conquer our fears and our stinginess and all the psychological gravity of our self-centeredness. And there are few joys, if any, greater than experiencing the liberating power of God's hospitality making us a new and radically different kind of people, who love to

reflect the glory of his grace as we extend it to others in all kinds of hospitality.[23]

In other words, hospitality is something we're made for. Every single person in our household is already hungry for purpose—including introverts like me. God wants us to relate to the wider world with hospitality. And the more we do, the more spiritually vibrant our home will become.

HOW CAN I PURSUE FOCUSED GROWTH IN THIS AREA?

It may be that God is calling you to focus on growing the spirituality or intimacy of your home right now. But if you sense God calling you to grow your home in hospitality, how can you pursue focused growth in this area? The following are a few resources that you might find helpful.

- "Open Doors: The Art of Hospitality." This online course explores what the Bible has to say about hospitality and provides helpful steps for discerning how your household can open its door a little wider. This free course includes helpful Scripture, insights from research, and various household interviews. This course can be found at www .lhm.org/households.

- Don Everts, *Go and Do: Becoming a Missional Christian* (Downers Grove, IL: InterVarsity Press, 2012). In this book I explore household service, personal evangelism, urban witness, church leadership and global crosscultural missions, exploring how we can live our lives on mission —whoever we are, whatever we do, and wherever we go.

- "Helping Your Child Welcome Others." Parents have high hopes for their children's faith, but they don't always know how to get them there. This booklet helps parents nurture a heart of hospitality within their child by walking through the biblical call to hospitality and giving examples of how children can respond to this call at home, in the neighborhood, at school, and at church. This booklet can be found at www.lhm.org/households.

- "Welcome." Hospitality is one of the best traits a child can learn, and this begins at home. This little booklet shows in words and pictures how important it is to be welcoming to others—just as God has invited and received us into his kingdom "home." This booklet can be found at www.lhm.org/households.

- "The Household Magnet." This magnet says "As for me and my household we will . . ." followed by plenty of space for your household to identify and record an area you want to focus on. (Like: "In February we will invite ten people over for a meal.") This magnet can live on your refrigerator as a reminder of what your household is focusing on and can be found at www.lhm.org/households.

CONCLUSION

WHEN DID I BECOME SO HOPEFUL ABOUT HOME?

It's been nine months now since Lilly's hopes and disappointment came streaming down her face and everyone in room 3205 grew quiet.

I was used to more clarity and fewer tears in class, and so I wondered, for a moment, what I had gotten myself into. I contemplated shuttering the whole messy experiment, but I'm glad we pressed on. I'm glad we continued the journey of exploring the home—a journey that brought us throughout the pages of the ancient Bible into the findings of the latest research and within the mysteries and tenderness of our own hearts.

For everyone in our learning lab it was quite a journey. We experienced paradigm shifts (*Who, exactly, is in my whole household?*), self-awareness (*Which of the three household habits is my household weakest in?*), scriptural insights (*Does God actually care about how my household prays together?*), and lots of practical steps (*For this week's homework assignment, strike up one deeper conversation in your home*).

And along the way there was lots of sharing and confessions and tender honesty. Lots of laughter and, yes, a few tears.

But here's the thing you need to know: there's nothing special about room 3205. Other than the three oversized, shapely windows that let in lots of sunlight, 3205 is pretty much like any classroom in any church you've been in. White walls and a mostly clean, thin carpet. A dry-erase board up front and a cart with Bibles in the back. The coffee people bring in from the lobby is pretty, well, *churchy* coffee.

There was nothing magical about our learning lab. Some weeks I was running in late because of other duties I was tending to in the church. Folks in the choir sometimes had to leave class early. Every now and then a baby wasn't feeling the nursery and so would join us in class and get bounced on daddy's knee at a back table.

And yet, I'll never forget that class.

I'll never forget the week Matt told us about how his homework assignment on prayer had gone. The assignment was to write a prayer that the family could use. Matt told us he decided to pen a unique prayer for each of his children. There were smiles (and a few sniffles) all around room 3205 as Matt told us how special his kids felt that they had their own special Daddy Prayer just for them! Matt told us how eager they each were at night to have their Daddy Prayer prayed over them before going to bed.

I'll never forget the lively discussion from the table of grand-parents who, emboldened by the news that people look to grandparents for spiritual coaching, started trying new things with their grandkids—and the grandkids were welcoming it.

We shared stories of inviting more people over, trying to start conversations, putting in place new rhythms. We found Christmas and Easter (actually Advent and Lent) to be great excuses for helping our households have more messy prayers and louder tables and wider doors.

I wish all of you could have been there the week Cypress sat up straight and declared, "Wait! So there really is a place for me? If I really am a member of these two extended households, that changes everything. Don, how can I take my role in the Everts household more seriously?"

No, I'll never forget that class. That class gave me hope.

It's not just the extraordinary nature of what God did among us that gives me such hope, it's the everyday, mundane context he did it within. It's the imperfect tools (like me) that he used to help us grow. That, I think, is part of what's making me so hopeful about homes these days.

Not just my own home (though I'm more hopeful about my own home than ever!) but homes everywhere. Even your home. I am hopeful that God can help you grow a more spiritually vibrant home!

I hope our prayers become a little messier, our tables a little louder, and our doors a little more open.

I hope we all experience the spiritual vibrancy God has for us and our homes.

You should know that's a lot of hope for an angsty member of Generation X to feel. But I suppose that's just a sign of how good God is at this whole household thing. He can even bring a conversation-avoiding nomad like me to a place of household hope.

May he do the same with you.

ACKNOWLEDGMENTS

As I finish this book my mind is casting back to all the folks I've had the honor of being at home with over the years—family, friends, housemates, extended household members, neighbors, guests. My gratitude for the gracious, forgiving, fascinating (and sometimes silly!) saints God has allowed me to live life with over the years is palpable. Thanks to all of you.

Special thanks to Wendy for so many reasons.

It continues to be a true honor and joy to be a part of the fruitful partnership that has blossomed between Lutheran Hour Ministries and the Barna Group. Both organizations are filled with bright, faithful, hard-working brothers and sisters, and I'm so thankful to be in the mix.

A final word of appreciation to the forty brave souls who joined me between September 2018 and May 2019 for the "Households of Faith" learning lab up in room 3205 at Bonhomme Presbyterian Church. Your questions and honesty and insights and grace and courage were a gift to me during our time together. I pray that in the pages of this little book I have faithfully offered them as a gift to many others.

RESEARCH PARTNERS

Barna Group

Barna Group (barna.com) is a research firm dedicated to providing actionable insights on faith and culture, with a particular focus on the Christian church. In its thirty-year history, Barna has conducted more than one million interviews in the course of hundreds of studies and has become a go-to source for organizations that want to better understand a complex and changing world from a faith perspective.

Lutheran Hour Ministries

Lutheran Hour Ministries (lhm.org) is a trusted resource in global media that equips and engages a vibrant volunteer base to passionately proclaim the gospel to more than 125 million people worldwide each week. Through its North American headquarters and thirty-four ministry centers on six continents, LHM reaches into more than fifty countries, often bringing Christ to places where no other Christian evangelistic organizations are present.

LHM and Barna are partnering together on a three-year research endeavor to reveal how Americans are expressing their faith. The first year of research looked at how individuals engage in spiritual conversations. The second year of research, which *The Spiritually Vibrant Home* is based on, focuses on the influence of households on spiritual development. The third year will look at the impact of Christians on the broader community. Don Everts is working with InterVarsity Press to produce a book based on each year of research.

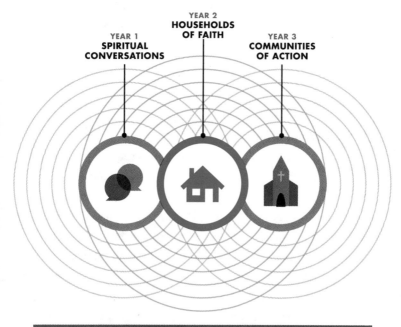

FIGURE 7.1

RESEARCH METHODOLOGY

This study began with in-depth qualitative interviews with highly active Christians of various household types: two nuclear families (white millennial parents with young children), one multigenerational family (Asian American household with children and boarders), one single-parent family (African American family that is sometimes multigenerational), and a roommate household (white millennial males). Key insights about what makes a vibrant household or how faith grows in a household setting were initially identified through this research.

The results from the qualitative interviews were used to shape the questionnaire for quantitative online surveys conducted from April 5–11, 2018. In total, 2,347 interviews were conducted, including 448 with teens between the ages of thirteen and seventeen. In order to qualify, respondents had to identify as Christian, agree strongly that their faith is very important in their life today, and report attending a church service at least once in the past month. The margin of error for the total sample is +/- 1.8 percentage points at the 95 percent confidence level.

Individuals living by themselves are excluded from this study. This sample is not designed to be representative of all household types in the United States. Because the goal of this study is to observe interactions among practicing Christians who live together and how faith is experienced and transmitted among them, households of a single person did not qualify for participation.

All research that seeks to capture the dynamics of a population has some inherent limitations but is useful to observe patterns and differences that reveal insights about the surveyed group. Online panelists are a collection of people who have pre-agreed to take surveys for some compensation, which may represent some motivational biases, so our surveys include quality control measures to ensure respondents are providing truthful and thoughtful answers to questions. When Barna samples from panels, respondents are invited from a randomly selected group of the US population for maximum representation. For this study researchers set quotas to obtain a minimum reasonable sample by household composition for statistical analysis. Additionally, quotas were set by a variety of demographic factors, and the data was weighted by ethnicity, education, region, and gender to reflect their natural presence among the practicing Christian segment.[1]

DEFINITIONS

T he following definitions are from "Households of Faith."[1]

GENERATIONS

Gen Z: born 1999 to 2015

Millennials: born 1984 to 1998

Gen X: born 1965 to 1983

Boomers: born 1946 to 1964

Elders: born in 1945 or earlier

HOUSEHOLDS

Nuclear family households include two married parents and their child(ren) under the age of eighteen. A second type, grown-up nuclear family households, includes two parents who live with only their adult child(ren).

Single-parent households include an unmarried parent and their child(ren) of any age. A single-parent household may also be a multigenerational household. Single parents who live with a partner are not included in this category.

Couple households include households with married couples who do not have children or anyone else living in the home.

Multigenerational households are composed of at least three generations in the home or a grandparent raising a grandchild. The household may also have nonfamily relatives living with them, such as borders or roommates, but these households do not overlap with roommate households.

Roommate households are made up of unmarried adults who share a home with a roommate or boarder.

Other households include teens or adults who live with another family member besides their parents, those who live with roommates but also live with a spouse and/or a child, or adults who live with their adult child and his or her spouse. All adults in this category do not fit into other categories defined above.

NOTES

INTRODUCTION: WHY DO WE GET SO EMOTIONAL ABOUT HOME?

[1]For more on this partnership, see "Research Partners" in appendix 1.

[2]Barna Group, *Households of Faith: The Rituals and Relationships That Turn a Home into a Sacred Space* (Ventura, CA: Barna Group, 2019).

1 HOMELIFE: RECOGNIZING THE SPIRITUAL SIGNIFICANCE OF THE MUNDANE

[1]Bill Bryson, *At Home: A Short History of Private Life* (New York: Anchor Books, 2010), 35.

[2]Bryson, *At Home*, 35-36.

[3]Bryson, *At Home*, 37.

[4]Bryson, *At Home*, 37.

[5]Craig G. Bartholomew, *Where Mortals Dwell: A Christian View of Place for Today* (Grand Rapids: Baker Academic, 2011), 112-13.

[6]H. Moxnes, *Putting Jesus in His Place* (Louisville: Westminster John Knox, 2003), 157, in Bartholomew, *Where Mortals Dwell*, 113.

[7]Simon K. Varghese, "The Church as the Household of God: A Biblical and Sociocultural Study" (PhD diss., Asbury Theological Seminary, 2005), 68.

[8]Varghese, "Church as the Household of God," 167.

[9]Michael F. Trainor, *The Quest for Home: The Household in Mark's Community* (Collegeville, MN: Liturgical Press, 2001), 15.

[10]David C. Verner, *The Household of God: The Social World of the Pastoral Epistles* (Chico, CA: Scholars Press, 1983), 1.

[11]Tish Harrison Warren, *Liturgy of the Ordinary* (Downers Grove, IL: InterVarsity Press, 2016), 34.

[12]Warren, *Liturgy of the Ordinary*, 24.

[13]Warren, *Liturgy of the Ordinary*, 22.

2 HOUSEHOLDS: UNPACKING
HOW THE BIBLE SEES OUR HOMES

[1]The average size of an American household is according to the 2010 United States Census. The average Israelite household is according to Brenda B. Colijn, "Family in the Bible: A Brief Study," *Ashland Theological Journal*, 2004, 73.

[2]Colijn, "Family in the Bible," 73.

[3]Simon K. Varghese, "The Church as the Household of God: A Biblical and Sociocultural Study" (PhD diss., Asbury Theological Seminary, 2005), 50, 53.

[4]Colijn, "Family in the Bible," 73.

[5]Colijn, "Family in the Bible," 73.

[6]David C. Verner, *The Household of God: The Social World of the Pastoral Epistles* (Chico, CA: Scholars Press, 1983), 9.

[7]Wayne A. Meeks, *The First Urban Christians: The Social World of the Apostle Paul* (New Haven, CT: Yale University Press, 2003), 75-76.

[8]Housing and domestic life underwent some changes. One recent excavation of a second-century Greco-Roman city (Ostia) revealed two basic types of housing used at the time: *domi* (which were like large private mansions that could house many people) and *insulae* (which were like multistoried apartment houses). This was new. But we should be careful not to assume these smaller individual apartments were like the insular houses we are accustomed to: it turns out most of these apartments were so small that they contained neither kitchens nor bathrooms, indicating that their residents "must have done most of their eating, drinking, and socializing in public spaces" (Verner, *Household of God*, 57).

[9]To explore this biblical theme of households and how they relate to your own current situation, use "Me and My Household," a free online course (www.lhm.org/households) that explores these issues and guides you in filling out your own complete household map.

[10]Barna Group, *Households of Faith: The Rituals and Relationships That Turn a Home into a Sacred Space* (Ventura, CA: Barna Group, 2019), 21.

[11]Ben Sasse, *Them: Why We Hate Each Other—and How to Heal* (New York: St. Martin's Press, 2018), 24.

[12]Sasse, *Them*, 26.

[13]E. Randolph Richards and Brandon J. O'Brien, *Misreading Scripture with Western Eyes: Removing Cultural Blinders to Better Understand the Bible* (Downers Grove, IL: InterVarsity Press, 2012), 100.

[14]Simon K. Varghese, "The Church as the Household of God: A Biblical and Sociocultural Study" (PhD diss., Asbury Theological Seminary, 2005), 42.

3 VIBRANCY: PULLING BACK THE CURTAIN
ON SPIRITUALLY VIBRANT HOMES

[1]A free PDF of this short history, "When God Shows Up On Campus," can be downloaded at www.lulu.com/shop/don-everts/when-god -shows-up-on-campus/ebook/product-17459553.html.

[2]See appendix 1, "Research Partners."

[3]See Barna Group, *Spiritual Conversations in the Digital Age: How Christians' Approach to Sharing Their Faith Has Changed in 25 Years* (Ventura, CA: Barna Resources, 2018); and my book based on the research, Don Everts, *The Reluctant Witness: Discovering the Delight of Spiritual Conversations* (Downers Grove, IL: InterVarsity Press, 2019).

[4]Barna Group, *Households of Faith: The Rituals and Relationships That Turn a Home into a Sacred Space* (Ventura, CA: Barna Group, 2019), 12.

[5]Barna, *Households of Faith*.

[6]Barna, *Households of Faith*, 12.

[7]Barna, *Households of Faith*, 24-25.

[8]Barna, *Households of Faith*, 19.

[9]See appendix 3, "Definitions," for a full generational breakdown.

[10]Rosaria Butterfield, *The Gospel Comes with a House Key: Practicing Radically Ordinary Hospitality in Our Post-Christian World* (Wheaton, IL: Crossway, 2018), 102.

[11]Barna, *Households of Faith*, 117, 122.

4 MESSY PRAYERS: HELPING OUR HOUSEHOLDS RELATE TO GOD

[1]Brenda B. Colijn, "Family in the Bible: A Brief Survey," *Ashland Theological Journal*, 2004, 74.

[2]Simon K. Varghese, "The Church as the Household of God: A Biblical and Sociocultural Study" (PhD diss., Asbury Theological Seminary, 2005), 53. Varghese points to several examples: Deuteronomy 4:9-10; 6:7, 20-25; 11:19; 32:46; Joshua 4:6-7.

[3]Varghese, "Church as the Household of God," 53.

[4]Colijn, "Family in the Bible," 74.

[5]Colijn, "Family in the Bible," 77.

[6]Barna Group, *Households of Faith: The Rituals and Relationships That Turn a Home into a Sacred Space* (Ventura, CA: Barna Group, 2019), 63.

[7]Barna, *Households of Faith*, 63.

[8]Barna, *Households of Faith,* 42.

[9]Kara E. Powell and Chap Clark, *Sticky Faith: Everyday Ideas to Build Lasting Faith in Your Kids* (Grand Rapids: Zondervan, 2011), 101.

[10]Barna, *Households of Faith*, 90.

[11]Barna, *Households of Faith*, 98.

[12]Douglas K. McKelvey, *Every Moment Holy* (Nashville: Rabbit Room Press, 2017).

[13]Colijn, "Family in the Bible," 73.

[14]Varghese, "Church as the Household of God," 70.

5 LOUD TABLES: HELPING OUR HOUSEHOLDS HAVE SPIRITUAL CONVERSATIONS

[1]Don Everts, *The Reluctant Witness: Discovering the Delight of Spiritual Conversations* (Downers Grove, IL: InterVarsity Press, 2019).

[2]Sherry Turkle, *Reclaiming Conversation: The Power of Talk in a Digital Age* (New York: Penguin Press, 2015), 4.

[3]Turkle, *Reclaiming Conversation*, 3.

[4]Wesley Hill, *Spiritual Friendship: Finding Love in the Church as a Celibate Gay Christian* (Grand Rapids: Brazos Press, 2015), 14.

[5]Hill, *Spiritual Friendship*, 56.

[6]Hill, *Spiritual Friendship*, 55.

[7]Jen Pollock Michel, *Keeping Place: Reflections on the Meaning of Home* (Downers Grove, IL: InterVarsity Press, 2017), 162.

[8]Barna Group, *Households of Faith: The Rituals and Relationships That Turn a Home into a Sacred Space* (Ventura, CA: Barna Group, 2019), 63.

[9]Barna, *Households of Faith*, 55.

[10]Barna, *Households of Faith*, 84-85.

[11]Barna, *Households of Faith*, 63.

[12]Barna, *Households of Faith*, 68.

[13]Barna, *Households of Faith*, 15.

[14]Barna, *Households of Faith*, 131.

[15]Barna, *Households of Faith*, 131.

[16]Barna, *Households of Faith*, 98.

[17]Barna, *Households of Faith*, 90.

[18]Barna, *Households of Faith*, 105.

[19]Barna, *Households of Faith*, 106.

[20]See Alan Kreider, *The Patient Ferment of the Early Church: The Improbable Rise of Christianity in the Roman Empire* (Grand Rapids: Baker, 2016).

6 OPEN DOORS: HELPING OUR HOUSEHOLDS EXTEND HOSPITALITY

[1]See, for example, M. P. Baumgartner, *The Moral Order of the Suburb* (Oxford: Oxford University Press, 1991).

[2]Lesslie Newbigin, *The Household of God: Lectures on the Nature of the Church* (Eugene, OR: Wipf & Stock, 1953), 13.

[3]For example, Rod Dreher, *The Benedict Option: A Strategy for Christians in a Post-Christian Nation* (New York: Penguin, 2017).

[4]Brenda B. Colijn, "Family in the Bible: A Brief Survey," *Ashland Theological Journal*, 2004, 79.

[5]Simon K. Varghese, "The Church as the Household of God: A Biblical and Sociocultural Study" (PhD diss., Asbury Theological Seminary, 2005), 60.

[6]W. E. Vine, *An Expository Dictionary of New Testament Words: With Their Precise Meanings for English Readers* (Old Tappan, NJ: Fleming H. Revell, 1940), 235.

[7]Jen Pollock Michel, *Keeping Place: Reflections on the Meaning of Home* (Downers Grove, IL: InterVarsity Press, 2017), 165.

[8]Rosaria Butterfield, *The Gospel Comes with a House Key: Practicing Radically Ordinary Hospitality in Our Post-Christian World* (Wheaton, IL: Crossway, 2018), 37.

[9]Butterfield, *Gospel Comes with a House Key*, 35.

[10]Barna, *Households of Faith: The Rituals and Relationships That Turn a Home into a Sacred Space* (Ventura, CA: Barna Group 2019), 27.

[11]Varghese, "Church as the Household of God," 78-79.

[12]John Piper, "Strategic Hospitality," *Desiring God* (blog), August 25, 1985, www.desiringgod.org/messages/strategic-hospitality.

[13]Barna, *Households of Faith*, 16.

[14]Frederick Buechner, *The Longing for Home* (San Francisco: HarperSanFrancisco, 1996), 139.

[15]Barna, *Households of Faith*, 42.

[16]This interdependence is exactly what we are to expect in the kingdom of God, according to Wesley Hill, who says, "Bent into a peculiar new configuration by the advent of Jesus and the descent of God's Spirit, friendship was now shaped by the cross and the empty tomb. No longer would believers gravitate only toward their social equals; now they would form committed, permanent relationships of affection that cut across lines of enslaved versus free, wealthy versus poor, highborn versus peasant" (Wesley Hill, *Spiritual Friendship: Finding Love in the Church as a Celibate Gay Christian* [Grand Rapids: Brazos Press, 2015], 57).

[17]Barna, *Households of Faith*, 83.

[18]Barna, *Households of Faith*, 17, 25.

[19]Hill, *Spiritual Friendship*, 114.

[20]Butterfield, *Gospel Comes with a House Key*, 31.

[21]Hill, *Spiritual Friendship*, 55.

[22]You can read about my hesitance to be involved in God's kingdom work (and God's successful efforts at wooing me to a life of purpose) in *Go and Do: Becoming a Missional Christian* (Downers Grove, IL: InterVarsity Press, 2012); and *The Reluctant Witness: Discovering the Delight of Spiritual Conversations* (Downers Grove, IL: InterVarsity Press, 2019).

[23]Piper, "Strategic Hospitality."

APPENDIX 2: RESEARCH METHODOLOGY

[1]Barna Group, "Households of Faith: The Rituals and Relationships That Turn a Home into a Sacred Space" (Ventura, CA: Barna Group, 2019), 151-52.

APPENDIX 3: DEFINITIONS

[1]Barna Group, "Households of Faith: The Rituals and Relationships That Turn a Home Into a Sacred Space" (Ventura, CA: Barna Group, 2019), 152-54.

ABOUT THE AUTHOR

Reverend Don Everts has worked with people of all ages and stages in life as an ordained pastor in the local church for over a decade. Don also worked with young adults for fourteen years on college campuses with InterVarsity Christian Fellowship. An award-winning author, he has written books for seekers and skeptics (including *Jesus with Dirty Feet*), for Christians who want to grow in their personal witness (including *The Reluctant Witness*), and for Christians who want to grow as disciples (including *The Smell of Sin*).

Don currently works with a team of writers, thinkers, educators, and leaders at Lutheran Hour Ministries to create cutting-edge, research-based, biblical resources that help equip Christians and churches everywhere to spread the good news around the world and in their own homes. More information on these resources can be found at www.lhm.org.

In terms of households, Don grew up in a nuclear household of five and has lived in a variety of roommate households over the years. Don and his wife, Wendy, have lived with several roommates and families over the years. They currently live in a wonderfully messy, multigenerational household in the St. Louis area with their three children (Simon, Teya, and Victor), Don's mother (Nancy), a dog that thinks he's a cat (ChiChi), and a cat that spends time in the neighborhood sewers (Penny).

OTHER TITLES FROM
LUTHERAN HOUR MINISTRIES

The Reluctant Witness
978-0-8308-4567-5

**The Hopeful
Neighborhood**
978-0-8308-4803-4

**The Hopeful
Neighborhood
Field Guide**
978-0-8308-4732-7

Discover Your Gifts
978-1-5140-0373-2

**Discover Your Gifts
Workbook**
978-1-5140-0449-4